Freehand
Graphics

Freehand Graphics

FOR ARCHITECTS, LANDSCAPE ARCHITECTS, AND INTERIOR DESIGNERS

A Problem-Solving Approach

Martha Sutherland

DESIGN PRESS

Thanks be to students, young and old
but ever new, who continuously
enrich the field of art.

First Edition, First Printing
Copyright © 1991 by Martha Sutherland
Printed in the United States of America
Designed by Ann Gold
Reproduction or republication of the content in any manner,
without the express written permission of the publisher, is
prohibited. The publisher takes no responsibility for the use of
any of the materials or methods described in this book, or for
the products thereof.

Library of Congress Cataloging-in-Publication Data
Sutherland, Martha
    Graphic fundamentals : freehand drawing for architecture
    architecture and interior design / Martha Clark Sutherland.
        p.   cm.
    Includes index.
    ISBN 0-8306-3480-0 : $14.95
    1. Architectural drawing—Technique.
    2. Free hand technical drawing—Technique. 3. Coordinates.
    4. Interior decoration—Design. I. Title.
    NA2708.S88   1991
    720′.28′4—dc20   90-21486
                                                           CIP

Design Press offers posters and The Cropper, a device for
cropping artwork, for sale. For information, contact Mail-
order Department. Design Press books are available at special
discounts for bulk purchases for sales promotions, fund raisers,
or premiums. For details contact Special Sales Manager.
Questions regarding the content of the book should be
addressed to:
    Design Press
    11 West 19th Street
    New York, NY 10011
Design Press books are published by Design Press, an imprint of
TAB Books. TAB Books is a Division of McGraw-Hill, Inc. The
Design Press logo is a trademark of TAB Books.

Contents

Preface

Students and practitioners of the spatial arts have a compelling need to be able to draw well. Architects, landscape architects, and interior designers all begin by creating a graphic image, freehand, on paper, just as in the end all these professionals use presentation sheets as a means of explaining and promoting their concepts. Even if presentations expand onto computer screens and develop into three-dimensional models, original concepts are still worked out on a piece of paper. Being able to record an idea quickly and accurately is an indispensable skill for designers.

Seeing accurately precedes drawing accurately. Not nearly as simple as most people tend to think, seeing accurately requires an objective view of the image in question: an ability to differentiate edges, to eliminate details, to respond to pattern. Art teachers have known for years that drawings most often reflect how we *think* objects appear, not how they actually appear. If we can create on paper the combination of lines, points, and values that the eye is truly seeing, the result will be pleasingly satisfactory and useful.

Although drawing is a practice-intensive skill, accurate observation is more than half the battle. Seeing accurately involves imposing some sort of order on the world we are viewing. As an ordering device, the grid is unsurpassed. All of the environment can be related to a grid, both two-dimensionally and three-dimensionally. Both flat and solid objects can be described on a two-dimensional surface using a grid. Moreover, buildings can be constructed of modules, which are a real-world three-dimensional grid.

We live in houses, drive on roads, plow fields, and read books whose skeletal nature is a gridded construct. Over our heads is an invisible pulsing checkerboard of electricity. Computers are digital grids of gigantic complexity. Every one of us can be located globally by a longitude and latitude grid system first conceived of by Ptolemy in A.D. 150.

Ten years of teaching have convinced me that an ability to relate the seen world to a grid increases objectivity in drawing, almost guaranteeing greater accuracy. Consequently, using grid paper as a sketching medium can provide a shortcut to more precise drawing, just as mental grids can clarify three-dimensional concepts.

Beyond this, a feel for contour can offer an insight into materials. Seeing negative space can create an appreciation for volumes. Practice in proportion will refine scale judgment. Exercises in all these concepts can improve visual acuity.

The wealth of problems and examples in this book are intended to make it easy for a student or practitioner to carry out a self-help program. Teachers can also use them to structure a studio class.

Among the difficulties facing a student, practitioner, or teacher is a lack of time to devote to necessary practice. Many an architecture school, for example, requires only one semester of freehand graphics, sometimes none. With such limited experience, students are supposed to be miraculously trained to transfer ideas from mind to paper with the flick of a pencil. A practice regime that applies methods used in art teaching to the types of drawings that are necessary to architecture, landscape architecture and interior design is a way of maximizing a limited amount of time.

This book is arranged with the easiest drawing systems—the orthographic ones—first. They include plans, elevations, and sections, the kinds of drawings that use no perspective. Skill in using the pencil and in accurate observation can be developed here before proceeding to the more demanding stage of perspective drawings. Finally, drawing from slides, still lifes, and nature is discussed.

Each section includes practice problems, created to engage the student on several levels: first, the mechanical one of understanding the appropriate drawing principle; second, the composition of the page, which should always be a consideration, and third, a design factor intentionally added wherever possible.

Freehand drawing skills *can* be improved, speeded up, made more accurate. The student examples in this book will attest to the results that are possible in the space of one three-month semester. All are by beginning students, most of them in a combined architecture, landscape architecture, and interiors studio, where exposure to the fundamentals of drawing for the professions and a core vocabulary are the same for all.

Problems

1. Non-representational composition of dots and straight lines
2. Non-representational composition of dots and straight lines forming right angles
3. Non-representational composition of dots and straight lines forming 45-degree angles
4. Composition of ten lines
5. Textured composition
6. First-floor plan of a house
7. Elevation of a street of houses
8. Elevation of a house facade
9. Drawing of a model elevation from memory
10. Interior elevation
11. Simple section drawing from a model
12. Site plan
13. Vertical section of map contours
14. Pattern practice
15. Pattern practice
16. Site plan rendered in ink
17. Site plan with model, rendered in ink
18. Trees rendered from a color photograph
19. Trees explored in a notebook
20. Isometric cube
21. Symmetrically dimetric cube
22. Unsymmetrically dimetric cube
23. Composition in paraline using letters
24. Four plan obliques
25. Ten exercises in descriptive geometry
26. Composition of ten solids
27. Casting a shadow from a wall in plan
28. Casting a shadow from a wall in plan
29. Casting shadows from walls of different heights
30. Casting shadows in elevation
31. Casting shadows in elevation
32. Shadows from a paraline box
33. Shadows from a paraline box
34. Casting shadows on a vertical surface
35. Casting shadows on a vertical surface
36. Casting shadows toward the viewer
37. Casting shadows from overhangs
38. Casting shadows from overhangs
39. Casting shadows on steps
40. Casting shadows on steps
41. Casting shadows on steps
42. One-point-perspective grid
43. Locating a box on a grid
44. Perspective of an irregular shape

1.

Graphic Fundamentals

This book about freehand graphics intended for students entering architecture, landscape architecture, and interior design programs. The drawing systems presented are the same as those used throughout professional schooling, even in hard-line drawing, which is drawing using a T square or a parallel bar and triangle. All of the exercises and problems in the book can be done without using straight-edged tools.

Students need to practice freehand drawing before beginning hard-line methods, as they quickly become dependent on straight-edged drawing tools and are loath to relinquish them, a habit that results in stiff and slow image making. Freehand drawing, on the other hand, encourages the blossoming of creative ideas out of quick and supple—albeit disciplined—exploratory sketching. Developing such a skill is the aim of this book.

DRAWING TOOLS AND EQUIPMENT

Drawing accurately, in a diagrammatic manner, is one of the most important habits a student can develop. Architecture, landscape architecture, and interior design are professions that call for a certain exactitude, even in quick sketching. The student is not looking at a future as an easel painter but as a designer, and the precise capturing of images is fundamental to all design disciplines.

Understanding the tools of the profession—the pencils, pens, paper, and erasers used in freehand drawing—is essential to mastering the skills of this drawing style.

For freehand drawing, nothing is as flexible, convenient, and forgiving as wooden pencils. Pencils are available in a range of hardnesses, from 6H (extremely hard leads) to 2H (hard leads) to F and HB at the middle of the scale to 2B (soft) to the extremely soft 6B (fig. 1-1). Pencils are manufactured beyond the 6H and 6B extremes, but they are for specialized work. Characteristically, soft pencils make rich dark lines and hard pencils make thinner silver gray ones. Ordinary yellow pencils are called number 2 pencils, and they are of a medium density, similar to an HB or F.

Lead holders, which click the lead out as you press on the end, are useful, but they are not supplied with the variety of leads available in wooden pencils.

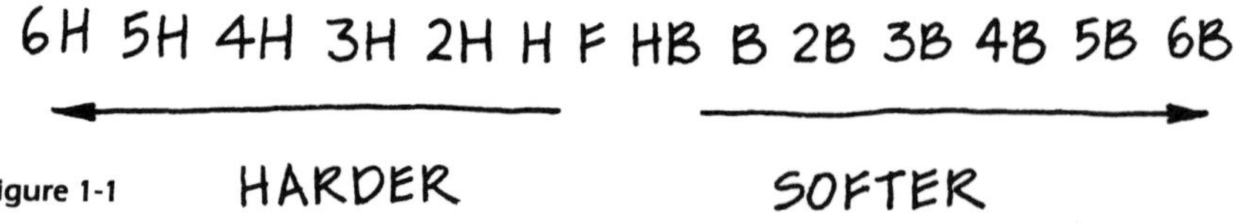

6H 5H 4H 3H 2H H F HB B 2B 3B 4B 5B 6B

Figure 1-1   **HARDER**   **SOFTER**

A wide variety of the pens on the market make excellent drawing tools. The familiar Pilot Fineliners and Razor Points are superb, but most of the fiber-tipped marker pens are good drawing tools. Ballpoint pens, however, should not be used, as they smear, skip, and produce an uneven line.

The paper of choice for studying freehand drawing is 8½- by 11-inch grid paper. The grid lines, light blue on a white page, will barely reproduce when photocopied. Manufactured primarily for engineers, this paper is available almost anywhere, under the name of quadrille paper or cross-section paper. The squares in the grid come in many sizes, such as one-quarter-inch squares, and one-eighth-inch squares, and in metric at 1 cm and 5mm. For the sketching problems in this book, the size of the squares is unimportant.

Architects use a lot of tracing paper because they are constantly changing technical drawings. Tracing paper varies according to quality. There are cheap pads of tracing paper that are almost like tissue paper, and at the other end of the spectrum, there is vellum, which is heavy, strong, and expensive. Vellum is called for in a few exercises in this book, as is some ordinary white paper of any type.

Except as noted otherwise in the Illustration Credits, the artwork in this book was done on 8½- by 11-inch sheets.

There are erasers of many kinds, but in general they fall into three categories: rubber, plastic, and kneaded. Pink Pearl is a good soft rubber eraser. Staedtler is a good soft plastic eraser. Soft as rubber and plastic are, however, they do ruffle the fibers of the paper somewhat, and an attempt to lay a very smooth layer of carbon on top of the erasure will betray the act underneath. A kneaded eraser, on the other hand, will lift off carbon without damaging the surface, making it the eraser of choice, since the name of the erasing game is to do the least possible damage to the surface of the paper. Pinch off a small amount of the kneaded eraser and press it against the paper, trying not to rub. After every pressing, knead the eraser. The eraser will absorb carbon until it is quite black. A kneaded eraser can also be shaped into a point to remove hard-to-reach penciling.

INTRODUCTORY PROBLEMS

Students often enter a drawing class with considerable anxiety about their ability; thus, it is wise to start with problems that do not call for realistic drawing. Straight-line exercises relieve tension, because the results are abstractions that need not "look like something."

The following introductory problems require large sheets of nongridded paper. The size allows the drawing of long lines—long enough for good practice as well as clear analysis.

First, an exercise: with a medium-soft pencil (F, HB, B), on a sheet of paper that is at least 10 by 14 inches (20 by 30 is best), make two dots, far apart. Connect them with a straight line, keeping the pencil on the paper; do not draw in fits and starts. Pull the line smoothly and at a medium pace. It is more important that the line be straight than that it meets the dot.

After a half dozen or so of these lines, try a different approach. Again make two dots, far apart; now fix your eye firmly on the second dot and pull your hand to it. Most people will feel that this is flying in the face of reason, but how do you know where you are going unless your eye is on the goal? Make enough lines to give this method a fair try.

Problem 1: Non-representational composition of dots and straight lines

Composition is another word for design. The types of composition are limitless, including symmetrical, asymmetrical, linear, curvaceous, strong, and weak. The quality of a composition depends on the nature of the problem.

This composition involves creating straight lines. Each line must be drawn by placing two dots far apart, one for the beginning and one for the end of the line. Remember that straight lines take attention and care; they do not just happen. Remember also to keep the lines long. Anyone can draw a straight line if it is short.

Begin the composition by simply drawing lines. When enough lines are on the sheet, some sort of a pattern will begin to emerge. More, rather than fewer, lines will enhance the composition. In fact, at the point when you are satisified with what is on the page, add ten more long lines. (See fig. 1-2.)

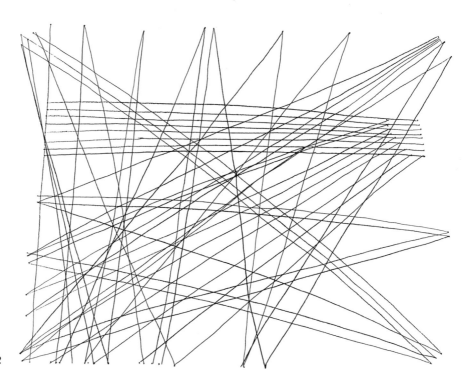

Figure 1-2

**Problem 2:
Non-
representational
composition of
dots and
straight lines
forming right
angles**

Right angles, or 90-degree angles, are perhaps the most commonly seen and drawn angles—we meet the ground at a right angle ourselves, as does almost every man-made object. Because they are so common, right angles are easily recognizable.

Place two dots on the page, far apart. Connect them with a straight line. Place another dot on the page and draw a line from it to the first line, at a right angle. Continue in this manner, with every new line meeting another at a right angle. Every now and then, check the accuracy of the angles against a corner of a piece of paper. An active effort must be made to keep the lines long, as there is a tendency to draw them shorter and shorter. When you feel the composition is complete, add ten more lines. (See fig. 1-3.)

**Problem 3:
Non-
representational
composition of
dots and
straight lines
forming
45-degree angles**

A 45-degree angle—half of a right angle—is not as instantly recognizable as the 90-degree angle. However, since drawing the right angle is easy, drawing half of a right angle should not be too difficult. Follow the same procedure as in problem 2, but draw every new line so that it meets another line at a 45-degree angle. Check the accuracy of the angles frequently against a corner of a piece of paper that has been folded in half diagonally. Again, when you deem the composition complete, add another ten lines. (See fig. 1-4.)

The success of these compositions lies in the straightness and the multiplicity of lines. In this case, less is *not* more.* Many more is better. Students will be satisfied with a composition long before the possibilities have been exploited.

There should be a critique after each problem. During a critique all the work is put up on the board and either the student or the instructor analyzes and evaluates it. It is an opportunity to comment on the straightness of the lines, to point out that dark lines carry better than light ones, and to discount drawings in which too many of the lines are too short.

A number of different composition styles will be represented. The most common will be the random or jackstraws pattern, in which the lines are distributed randomly but evenly. There will be symmetrical arrangements, geometrical ones, compositions that convey a three-dimensional effect, others that have a focal point, and even some that look like some object, though the instructions should have forbidden realism. None of these is necessarily better than the others; each is simply different. What is important is the quality of the line, as well as the feeling of the composition—energetic, placid, strong, directed, weak, wobbly. There will be interesting differences among the three compositions in terms of the feelings they convey. The 45-degree-angle problem will probably appear more spiky than the others, whereas the right-angle problem is open to geometric compositions.

Critiques are valuable teaching devices through which students learn as much from their peers as from the instructor. Critiques are a standard practice in architectural schools, and it is worthwhile for students to become familiar with the procedure, to know how to describe their own work, how to speak to the viewers, and how to reply to criticism.

*The great architect Mies van der Rohe made the often-quoted remark, "Less is more."

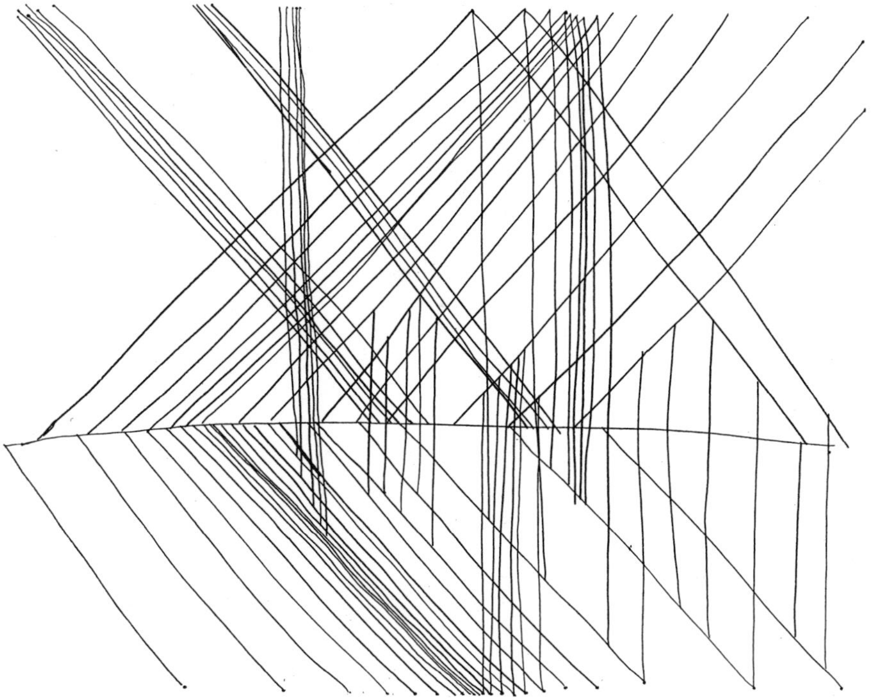

Figure 1-3

Figure 1-4

The next set of problems requires a pen. A policy of frequently shifting to ink will take the fear out of working in this nonerasable medium.

Pen has many advantages over pencil in freehand drawing. It eliminates the pale look, it saves time spent in endless erasing, and it makes the author of the line more careful. Perhaps most important, it gives a line conviction.

These problems will also introduce the use of gridded paper. A grid is a scheme into which one inserts chaos and derives order. This happy result is dear to the human heart because it creates the illusion that we have control over ourselves and our environment. Order is easier to understand and more comforting than disorder, in drawing as in other areas of life. Graphics are produced more easily, more quickly, and more accurately in an orderly fashion than they are in an intuitive one. Most of the student drawings in this book were done on gridded $8^1/2$- by-11-inch paper and were accomplished in less time and with more confidence than similar drawings that did not make use of such an aid. Does dependency on a grid develop? Not at all. Students do not even seem to notice when another kind of paper is used.

The simplest grid is a single-order spatial system formed of a series of lines intersecting at 90-degree angles at regular intervals, which is what a pad of quadrille paper is. Additionally, it comes in the very handy $8^1/2$- by-11-inch size. The small format of the sheet is advantageous in that it allows for speedy drawing; moreover, architects work to a small scale more frequently than to a large one.

Problem 4: Composition of ten lines

With a pen on gridded paper, draw a border close to the edge of the paper, following the grid lines. Within the border make a composition of ten lines, each of which must extend from one border line to any other border line. The composition can be formal or asymmetrical, though formal often translates as dull. Each line should be carefully considered before being drawn. Diagonal lines project more vitality and spirit than orthographic (right-angled) lines. As in the earlier problems, strive for straight lines. (See fig. 1-5.)

In a classroom situation, this problem should be followed by a critique. Again, the compositions will show clear differences, which can be used to frame a discussion about balance, repetition, texture, and other components of interesting design.

Problem 5: Textured composition

Using a pen, convert the linear composition from problem 4 into textured planes by filling in as many spaces as desired with straight, parallel lines. Use insights gleaned from the critique to create the new composition. The lines may go in any direction and be any distance apart, but must be parallel within each plane. The planes left untouched should be considered in the same way as the textured ones, because they also form the composition.

As spaces are filled in, become an active participant in the new creation. Make it do what you want it to do. It will be an entirely new product. If the original design lacked pep or content, invigorate it here. Do not neglect the effort to keep lines straight. (See fig. 1-6.)

There are many possible variations on this problem: the planes can be filled with crosshatch, curved lines, or dots instead of parallel lines; color can also be introduced.

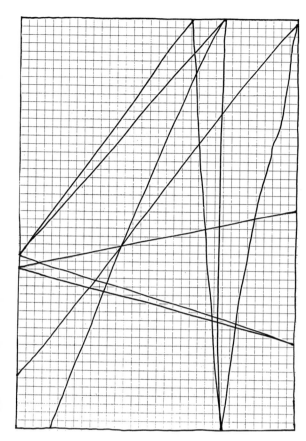

Figure 1-5

Figure 1-6

2.

Orthographic Projections

Practicing the drawing of straight lines is an overture to the production of orthographic drawings. Plans, elevations, and sections are the three types of orthographic drawings, views of the world without perspective. The word *orthographic* refers to right angles. The word projection refers to the rules by which the drawing is constructed.

Orthographic views are used by designers as working drawings for contractors and the like. They will eventually be produced in final form with a T square or parallel bar and a triangle, but quick freehand plans and elevations almost always form the first tentative design concepts.

Orthographic views are easy to draw, relying almost exclusively on straight lines and a modicum of skill in pencil technique. Because not much practice is required to learn about the projections, fewer problems are included in this section. Skill can be developed by beginning with these drawings and progressing through paralines and perspectives, so that the more challenging drawing from slides and nature that follow will seem less formidable.

In orthographic projections surfaces that are parallel to the drawing paper are shown head on. In more exact terms, all visible points on a structure are projected onto the picture plane at a 90-degree angle.

PLANS

Of all the orthographic views, plans are the most diagrammatic, thereby requiring the least drawing skill in the preliminary stage. A plan is in fact a horizontal section. Imagine that a giant blade has sliced horizontally through your house, cutting it off at the knees—actually at a level of 3 or 4 feet. Everything above the slice has been thrown away. The walls that are left show the voids of doors and the position of windows (fig. 2-1).

Because buildings are by and large composed of right angles—a function of materials and statics—grid paper is a great convenience in drawing plans of them, allowing scale to be considered from the very beginning. A dimension can be assigned to the squares and used to estimate size.

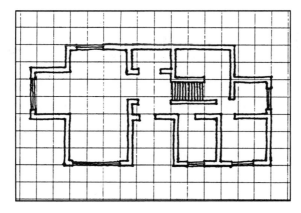

**Problem 6:
First-floor plan
of a house**

Using a medium pencil and grid paper, work out the first-floor plan of your own house or apartment. Assign a size to the squares of your grid and using whatever approximate scale you can devise, attempt to fit the rooms together.

When you have a sketch that seems reasonable, redraw the plan on a new sheet of grid paper, using double lines for walls, leaving a space for doors, and showing windows with three parallel lines.

Plans can indicate general context too. Frequently called a *footprint*, the line where the structure touches the ground shows the structure in context with its surroundings. Whereas plans can show the first floor, second floor, roof, and the like, a footprint is only the outline of wall in contact with earth.

Plans illustrate such important concerns as relationships of spaces and traffic patterns, but they give little information about the way a structure will look. Consequently, elevations and perspectives are needed to support plans.

ELEVATIONS

Elevations are used to add information that plans fail to supply. They also make attractive graphics that can charm with their clean, crisp appearance.

An elevation of a building is drawn as though every inch of the facade is being seen dead on. No perspective is conveyed. The term *elevation* is almost always applied to manmade structures. Trees, people, landscapes, and other natural objects are not described as being in elevation. Instead, when viewed straight on, these are described as being seen in one-point perspective.

The purpose of an elevation, either exterior or interior, is to create a schema of the vertical planes, showing the division of spaces, perhaps textures, and sometimes even construction techniques. Such things as fenestration patterns (shape, size, and placement of windows), spacing of columns, and the balance of parts are shown clearly in an elevation.

Drawing elevations offers an opportunity to practice judging proportions, sizes, and shapes.

Figure 2-2

**Problem 7:
Elevation of a
street of houses**

A whole street's worth of elevations is a wonderfully instructive effort and results in an in-depth understanding of the personality of a neighborhood—its scale, period, economic status, and ethnicity.

Using a pencil and grid paper, draw an elevation based on a row of houses along a street. Sit across the street from each house as you draw. The grid squares can be assigned a value of 2 feet, 3 feet, or more, depending on how detailed the drawing will be. Estimate the heights of the houses by comparing them to a person walking by, who shall be assumed to be 6 feet tall. Slope of the terrain can frequently be judged against the line of the house foundation. When all the houses have been drawn, redraw them carefully in ink. The final drawings can be assembled to make an attractive frieze. (See fig. 2-2).

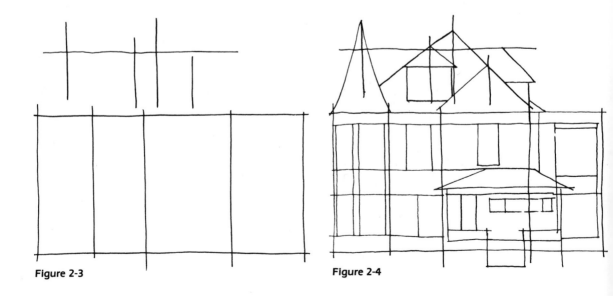

Figure 2-3   Figure 2-4

**Problem 8:
Elevation of a
house facade**

To produce more careful elevations, use the grid paper to divide the facade of the building, based on its major areas of definition.

Use a pencil and grid paper. Pick a house with an interesting facade. Working always from the large to the small, graphically answer the following questions. What is the overall shape of the facade? Where is the ridge line? The tops of the windows? Consider each element of the facade—its place and purpose within the design. The skeleton can be laid out quickly; after that the details can be tackled. (See figs. 2-3, 2-4, and 2-5).

The elevations in figures 2-6 and 2-7 were done by students in a graphic fundamentals class, using grid paper.

**Problem 9:
Drawing of a
model elevation
from memory**

Working from memory forces you to consider the whole structure, reducing the distractions of details. A building model or a large photograph of a building elevation is placed behind a screen or in another room. View the model and then return to the drafting table to begin drawing. It is remarkable how memory improves after innumerable trips.

Use a pencil and grid paper. Look at the model carefully, memorizing first its basic rectangular shape and then the major divisions of its construction. Run to your drawing table to put down as much as you can remember. Only after the basics have been successfully transferred to your paper should you proceed to such elements as roof pitch and large windows. (See fig. 2-8.)

Figure 2-5

ORTHOGRAPHIC PROJECTIONS | 21

Figure 2-6

Figure 2-7

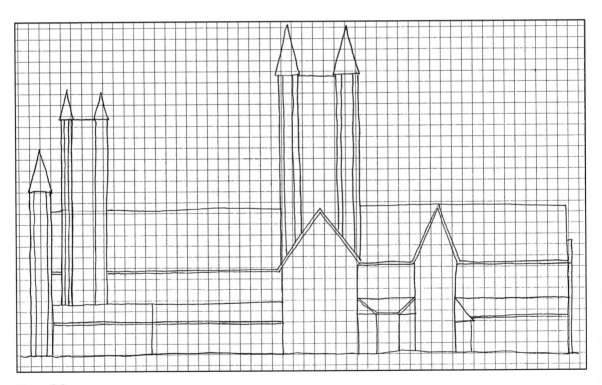

Figure 2-8

INTERIOR ELEVATIONS

Interior elevations show the relationships among doors and wall space, room dividers, shelves, built-in furniture and appliances, and other permanent interior elements.

Problem 10:
Interior elevation

Use a pencil and grid paper. Situate yourself looking straight at an interesting interior wall. Assign a scale to the squares on your gridded page—one square equals 6 inches, for example—and use that as a quick guide to the size of the wall. Estimate the height of the wall from a human figure (yourself or another) and other vertical measurements by subdividing the figure height. Determining horizontal measurements involves judging proportions. Draw the elevation and include a human figure for scale. (See fig. 2-9.)

Practice by eyeballing interesting walls anywhere. Wait until a person goes by so that you can compare and estimate sizes based on the approximate 5 to 6 feet of the person's height, and structure everything according to this measure. (See fig. 2-10.)

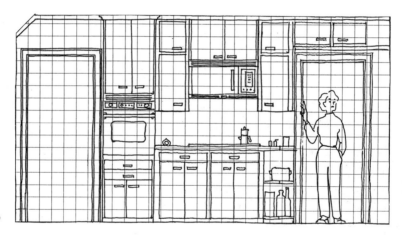

Figure 2-9

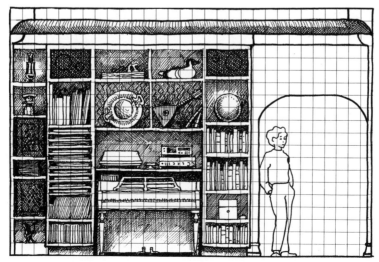

Figure 2-10

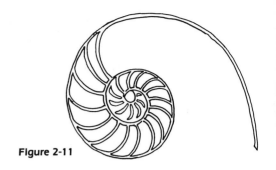

Figure 2-11

SECTIONS

A section of a building is a vertical slice through the structure, taken as though a guillotine had chopped it. You may be familiar with a section of a nautilus shell (fig. 2-11) or with do-it-yourself section diagrams (fig. 2-12).

In a section, everything on the near side of the cut is removed. In a building section, the cut edges are always shown outlined with a very heavy line, or sometimes filled in. The filling is called *poché* (poh-shay) by architects. Cut sections of beams are shown with intersecting diagonal lines, forming an X. The rest of the building beyond the cut line is drawn as an elevation (fig. 2-13).

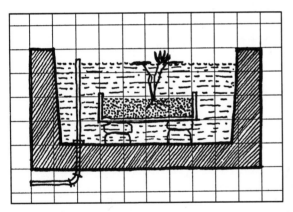

Figure 2-12

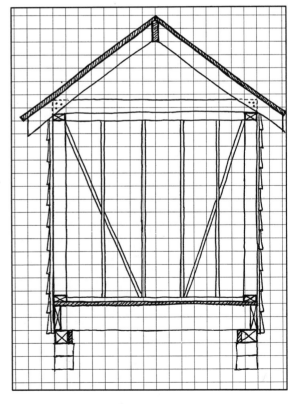

Figure 2-13

Sections are diagrams—frequently of considerable importance—and although usually they are eventually prepared as hard-line drawings (drafted with a T square or parallel bar and a triangle), several freehand sketches can quickly and easily establish a desirable point of view.

Architects use sections to explain how buildings fit together. Landscape architects take vertical sections to show ground contours. Sections are used by interior designers to show the view of a room and by industrial designers to describe the inner workings of a product.

Models make good subjects for drawing sections because they are simple and do not require much knowledge about engineering and construction.

**Problem 11:
Simple section
drawing from a
model**

Use a pencil and grid paper. Decide where the section is to be cut, and then mentally work out which solid areas will be cut. Draw the cut lines double, and fill them in, to make sure that they are heavy enough. Figures 2-14 and 2-15 show an elevation and a section drawn by a student from a model.

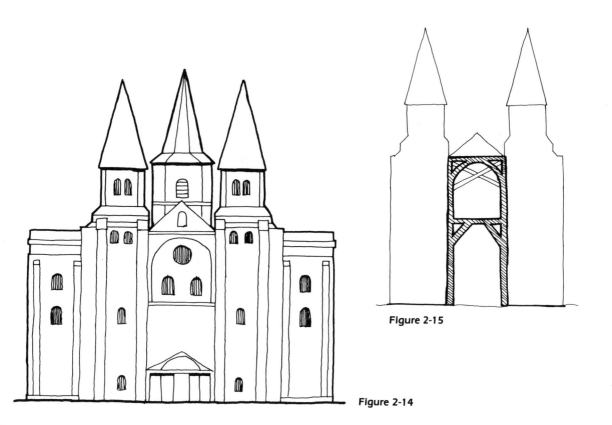

Figure 2-15

Figure 2-14

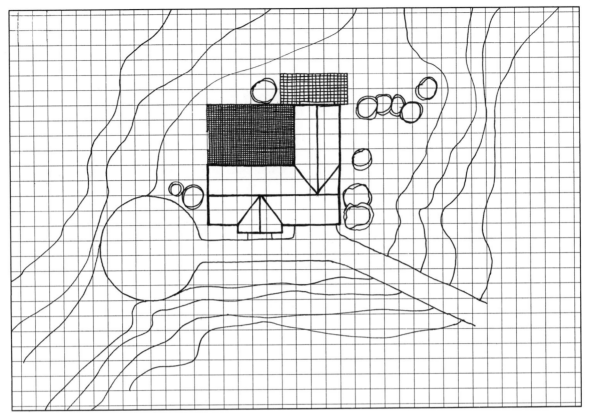

Figure 2-16

SITE PLANS AND MAP CONTOURS

A site plan is an aerial view of an expanse of ground, including possible structures (fig. 2-16). It is used to show relationships among buildings, parking lots, access roads, gardens, ground contours, and other exterior elements. A site plan may show the roof details of any buildings that are included.

**Problem 12:
Site plan**

Use a pencil and grid paper. Assign a scale to the squares of your gridded paper, one square equals 2 feet, for example. Devise a simple plan that includes a small rectangular house, 30 by 40 feet, with an attached garage of 12 by 18 feet. Draw in a driveway and a front walk. Outline flower beds and a small terrace. Draw the outline of the house and garage with a heavy, dark line and the other outlines lighter and thinner.

Map contours are horizontal sections cut at a specified number of feet above a base measurement. In a drawing each contour line (section) is the outline of a certain height, which is indicated at each side of the drawing (fig. 2-17).

A contour map shows heights and depths graphically, but it is difficult to visualize just *how* steep or *how* flat the contours are. A quick route to enlightenment is to prepare a vertical section.

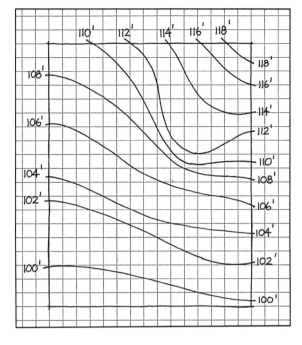

Figure 2-17

Problem 13:
Vertical section
of map contours

Use a pencil and grid paper. Copy the contours of figure 2-17 or devise your own. Visualize what the contour lines mean physically—what the heights and depths would look like in three dimensions. A contour map is a series of piled-up horizontal sections. (See fig. 2-18.)

Visualize taking a vertical section through the horizontal sections (fig. 2-19).

In plan, the arrows on the cut line show in which direction one is looking. The rest of the drawing is removed (fig. 2-20).

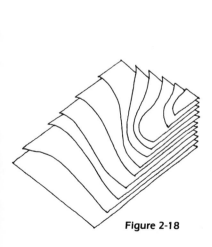

Figure 2-18

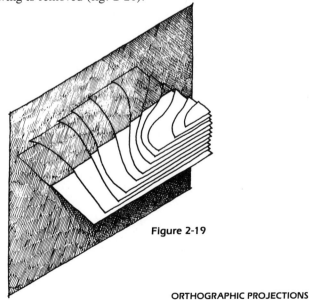

Figure 2-19

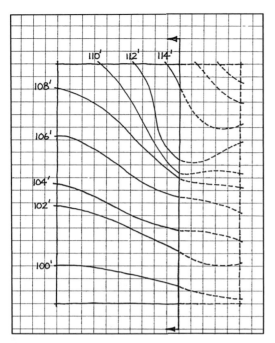

Figure 2-20

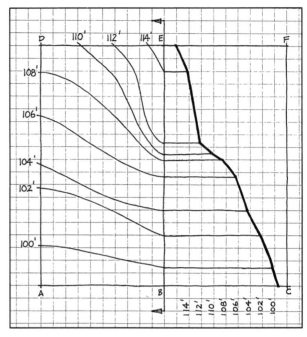

Figure 2-21

To draw a vertical section, label the lower left corner of the contour drawing as point A, the upper left corner as point D, the intersection of the cut line with the lower boundary of the drawing as point B, and the intersection of the cut line with the upper boundary of the drawing as point E. Extend line AB some distance to the right, to point C. Extend line DE the same distance to the right to point F. Draw line CF. (See fig. 2-21.) Rotate the page so that line CF is horizontal, and tick off a graph along the cut line, BC, to represent 2-foot vertical increments. The graph should correspond to the grid lines. Extend vertical parallel lines from the intersections of the section lines and the cut line to the appropriate height lines, found on the graph.

The horizontal distance of the contour map should agree in scale with the vertical rise. In creating a section like this, however, the rise of the ground in proportion to the distance covered will almost surely result in a very flat topographical representation. Vertical exaggeration is therefore used. In a freehand drawing, the vertical exaggeration is automatically incorporated, since the graph lines must be far enough apart to see.

Figure 2-22 shows a site plan and section of the water garden cascades of the sixteenth-century Villa Torlonia, near the city of Frascati, in Italy.

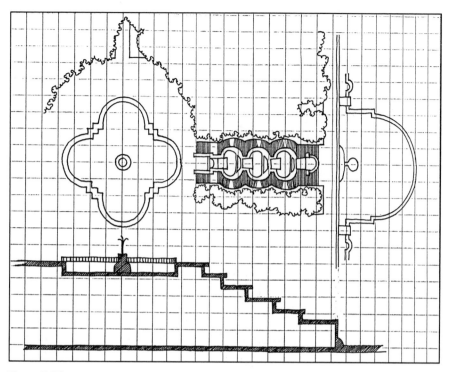

Figure 2-22

RENDERING PLANS AND SITE PLANS

After so much straight-line drawing, it is time for a change of pace. In the development of any site plan or elevation, the rendering of the various elements is important to the finished product. To produce an accurate graphic, you must master a vocabulary of freehand symbols for trees and shrubs, ground covers, water, and building materials such as brick, tile, wood, and stone. The symbols can range from abstract to stylized to realistic, as you wish, but they must be consistent throughout a drawing. Symbols are nothing but patterns, repeated over and over. They require practice.

Grade contours can be represented by simple straight lines, angled to fit the curves. Straight lines will create the impression that the contours are some sort of grassy lawn, pasture, or even bare slope (figs. 2-23 and 2-24).

Ground covers are indicated with an overall pattern, random or geometric. There may be a need for four or five different types in one drawing, so a variety is necessary. The following are some common means of representing ground covers:

- Individual plants drawn close together (fig. 2-25)
- A continuous line squiggle, drawn without lifting the pencil (fig. 2-26)
- An angular squiggle that does not overlap (fig. 2-27)
- Rosettes (fig. 2-28)
- Continuous arcs (fig. 2-29)

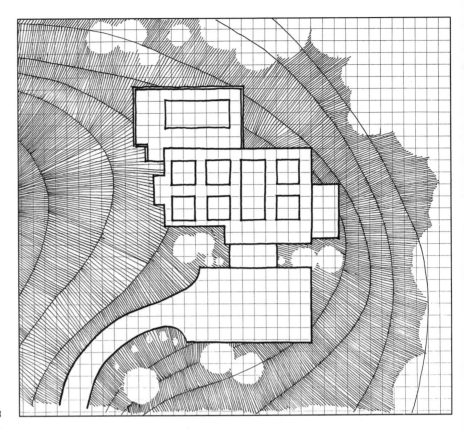

Figure 2-23

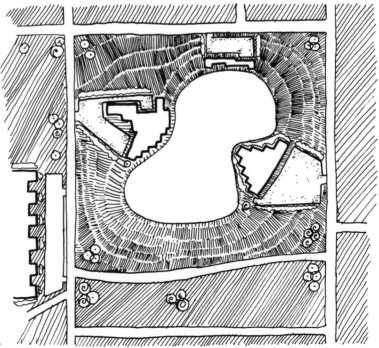

Figure 2-24

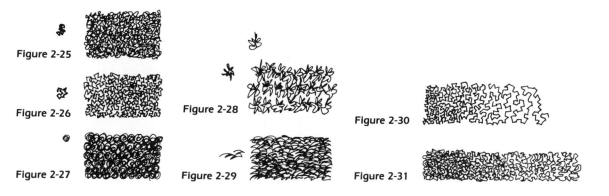

Figure 2-25

Figure 2-26

Figure 2-27

Figure 2-28

Figure 2-29

Figure 2-30

Figure 2-31

Problem 14:
Pattern practice
Use a pen and plain white paper. Draw several long rectangles. Fill each with a different random pattern, concentrating on a smooth progression from dense to thin. (See figs. 2-30 and 2-31.)

Problem 15:
Pattern practice
Using a pen and grid paper, copy the garden design in figure 2-32 onto gridded paper, and fill in the spaces with appropriate patterns. The plan is of the gardens of the sixteenth-century Villa Pallavicini near Frascati, Italy.

Tile, brick, and concrete block, in plan, are drawn as simple grids. Figure 2-33 shows brick on edge; figure 2-34, brick face; and figure 2-35, flagstone.

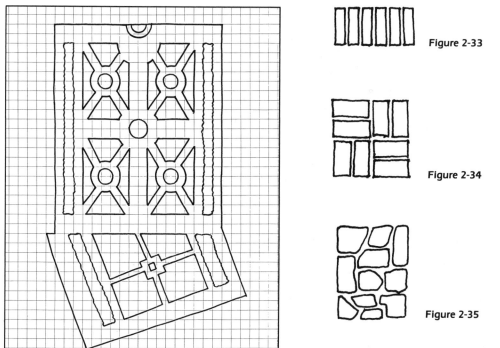

Figure 2-33

Figure 2-34

Figure 2-35

Figure 2-32

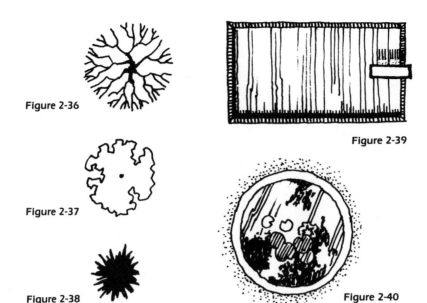

Figure 2-36

Figure 2-37

Figure 2-38

Figure 2-39

Figure 2-40

Trees are one of a miscellaneous collection of objects called *entourage*. The term is applied to landscaping plants, important trees, garden furniture, water fountains, doghouses, and other elements that support the design of a structure. Trees are drawn to show the extent of their canopy, which can be represented as a simple circle or something quite complex. In freehand drawing, perfect circles are hard to come by. Going around the circle twice to feather the edge a little will help.

Deciduous trees are frequently drawn bare of leaves so that some of the ground shows through (fig. 2-36). Divide and subdivide the branches as they reach the canopy edge. If the tree is drawn as a solid, the edges should be crimped in an interesting way (fig. 2-37). A dot in the center may make it look less like a map of Antarctica. Conifers are spiky, filled-in circular shapes, like ink blots (fig. 2-38).

Water can be difficult to represent. Use straight lines if the water is still, and dark shadows to suggest reflections (figs. 2-39 and 2-40).

**Problem 16:
Site plan
rendered in ink**

Use a pen and grid paper. Using the preceding inventory of symbols, as well as other symbols that you devise, lay out a plan of a simple walled garden and fill in the areas with appropriate patterns. The universal symbol for gravel is lots of tiny dots. (See fig. 2-41.)

**Problem 17:
Site plan with
model, rendered
in ink**

Use a pen and grid paper. This is a more ambitious plan. Choose a model of a building or a church to use as the core of the plan. Around it devise driveways, parking areas, formal gardens, and other landscape elements. Render the areas with appropriate patterns. (See figs. 2-42 and 2-43.)

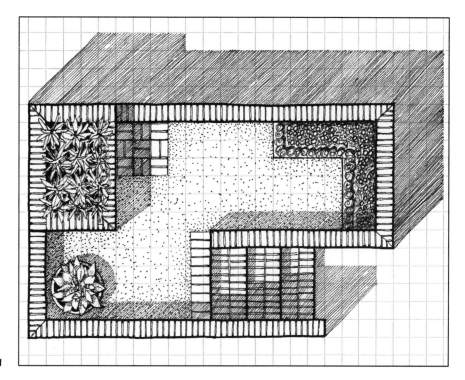

Figure 2-41

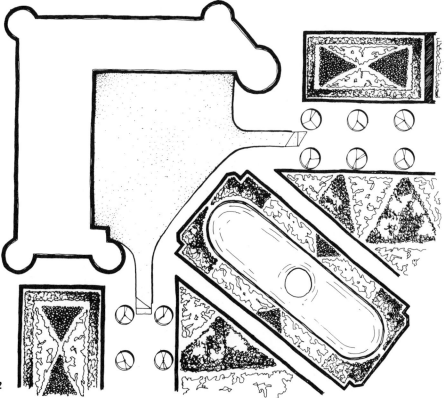

Figure 2-42

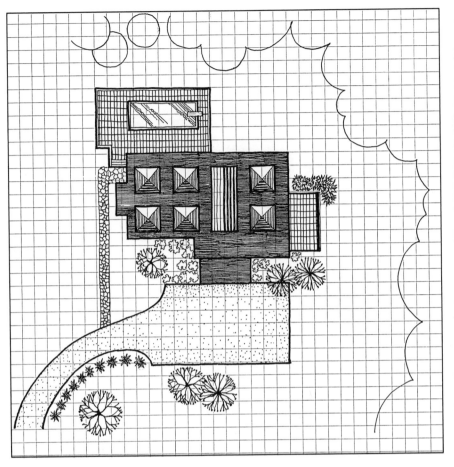

Figure 2-43

RENDERING ELEVATIONS

The patterns and pencil strokes used in rendering elevations are similar to those for site plans, but there are more of them. They require practice.

Ground covers—grass, ivy, and the like—can be represented in the following ways:

- A series of round-topped lines, which look like m's, with the height and the direction of the strokes varied a bit (fig. 2-44)
- A series of pointy-topped lines, resembling u's or v's, which are variations of the m's (fig. 2-45)
- A combination of m's and u's (fig. 2-46)
- Round squiggles that look like plants (fig. 2-47)
- Pointy squiggles that look like plants (fig. 2-48)

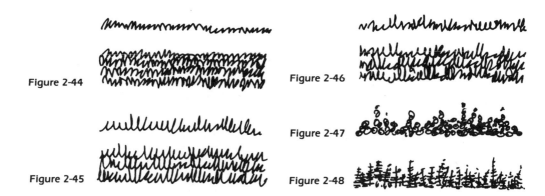

Figure 2-44

Figure 2-45

Figure 2-46

Figure 2-47

Figure 2-48

Trees do not have perspective in the usual sense of the convergence of parallel lines, and so the same techniques used in elevation graphics can be adapted to the rendering of trees anywhere. Three handsome examples, executed by beginning landscape architecture students, are shown in figures 2-49, 2-50, and 2-51. They are all different but serve to show how expressive the simple graphic code can be. The source for these drawings was a color photograph.

Figure 2-49

Figure 2-50

Figure 2-51

Problem 18:
Trees rendered
from a color
photograph

Use a pen and plain white paper for this problem. Find a color photograph of a for-est or other dense tree-scape. Using the preceding vocabulary of plan and elevation graphics, render the tree shapes in ink, showing differences in color by using differ-ent symbols.

Trees are vital pieces of entourage, the rendering of which can make or break the appearance of a presentation. In style, they fall into three categories: abstract, sim-plified, and realistic. They can also be positive (dark against a light background) or negative (light against a dark background).

Abstract trees are geometrical—round, triangular, oval, and polygonal (fig. 2-52). Abstractions are the easiest and the least aesthetic of possible solutions. They do nothing to produce a sympathetic ambience or to enhance the design they sup-port.

Simplified trees are a more satisfactory solution (fig. 2-53). They can suggest the species of the tree; they can complement the structure; they can be beautiful.

Realistic trees, being the most difficult to draw, can be a wonderful addition to a rendering if handled skillfully but can be disastrous if rendered poorly. Care must be taken not to create such beautiful trees that the structure they are meant to support is overwhelmed. The degree of realism to incorporate is also a consideration, depen-dent on the style of the rendering as a whole and the skill of the artist.

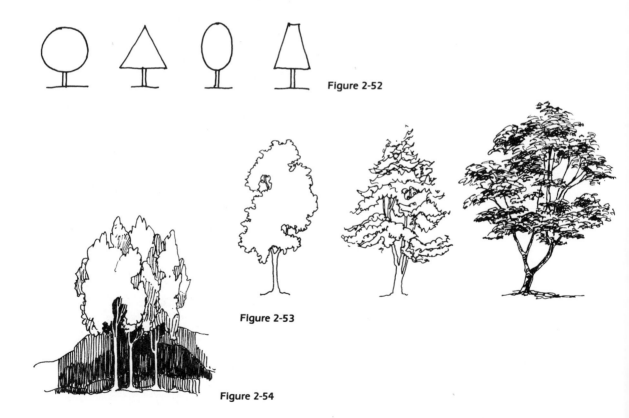

Figure 2-52

Figure 2-53

Figure 2-54

**Problem 19:
Trees explored in
a notebook**

Using a pencil or pen and a small sketch pad or notebook, spend time drawing trees from life. First, check the abstract shape, and lightly pencil it in. Notice which side is getting the sun so that you can darken the appropriate side of the trunk and extend a shadow along the ground. Remember that there will always be shadow under the canopy. Use a pattern for the foliage that best interprets the species of tree. Is the foliage thick, thin, dark, light? Consider the leaf pattern—is it tiny and flickering or dense and featureless? Is it clumpy or stringy? Pursue the nature of the tree as you would pursue a beguiling member of the opposite sex. The pleasure of winning a victory over the technical difficulties is very sweet.

Figure 2-54 is an example of simplified trees. Outlined shapes preserve a decorative quality without being too specific and pushy. You do not want more attention paid to the entourage than to the structure. Notice how attractive light trees are against a dark background. Figures 2-55, 2-56, 2-57, and 2-58 are examples of trees by students in both pencil and pen. Entourage in elevation, rendered by a landscape student, is shown in figures 2-59, 2-60, and 2-61. The landscape components, including benches, drinking fountains, and signage, that may be only entourage in an architectural drawing may well be the primary subjects of a landscape plan, and should be handled accordingly. Simple shape and style are appropriate for entourage; the elements should be as detailed as necessary in a landscape plan.

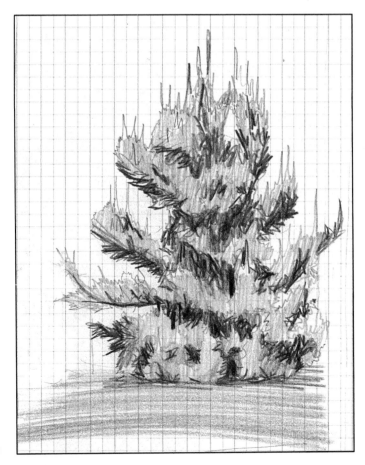

Figure 2-55

Figure 2-56

Figure 2-57

Figure 2-58

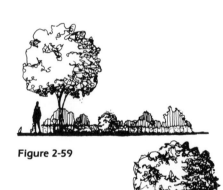

Figure 2-59

Figure 2-60

Figure 2-61

3.

Paraline Drawings

Paraline drawings show three faces of an object at one time, unlike orthographic drawings, which show only one. In a paraline drawing, all lines that are parallel on the object are parallel in the drawing. Because all parallel lines can be measured and then drawn to scale, paraline drawings are very easy to construct and to draw.

Paraline drawings are popular because they are an easy way to make an object look three dimensional. They suffer, however, from a monumental disadvantage: they are distorted. We do not see the world in paraline; we see it in perspective. Paraline drawings do not sell work, for the very good reason that they look odd. They are distorted just enough to make the average viewer think something is wrong—a state of affairs that does not instill confidence in the client. Nevertheless, paraline drawings are widely used in architectural schools, because they provide a quick and easy way to judge three dimensions.

All paraline drawings have one thing in common: they use parallel lines in the drawing to represent parallel lines in the object. They differ, however, in viewpoint. The choice of which paraline type to use is made by virtue of what needs to be shown in the drawing.

Paraline is the family name of drawing types that include:

- Axonometrics, which are subdivided into *isometrics* and *dimetrics*, which are further subdivided into *symmetrical* and *unsymmetrical dimetrics*
- Obliques, which are subdivided into *plan obliques* and *elevation obliques*

AXONOMETRICS: ISOMETRICS AND DIMETRICS

Isometric drawings are oriented in such a way that three planes are visible and at their intersection all three angles are equal. The object viewed isometrically can be tipped in several directions, but the angles must remain the same. Observe that in all four views in figure 3-1, the boxes are identical.

Isometric drawings are frequently used in product design because they can clarify shapes and relationships and they can be drawn to scale (fig. 3-2). Architects for years have been in the business of designing things like tea sets and pencil sharpeners and chess men, all of which can be diagramed efficiently isometrically. Furniture design is another field in which architects and landscape architects alike have made their mark. Isometric drawings are particularly useful for chairs and tables.

Problem 20:
Isometric cube

Using a pencil and grid paper, draw an isometric cube. Start by drawing a vertical line for the near edge. At the bottom of the line, estimate two 30-degree angles against the horizontal. Use the diagonal of the grid square—which divides the right angle into two 45-degree angles—to estimate the 30-degree angles. Duplicate the angles at the top of the vertical line. Add the remaining lines to form a cube, parallel to the existing lines.

Practice in estimating angles can result in remarkably accurate freehand drawings.

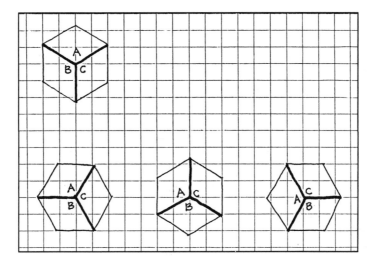

Figure 3-1

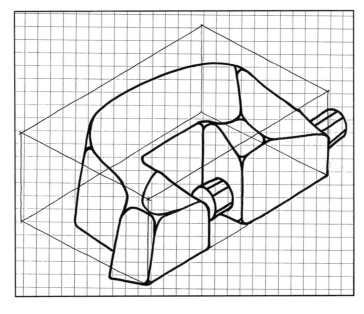

Figure 3-2

Dimetric drawings are oriented in such a way that two axes form the same angle with the picture plane, while the third is different. If the angles against the horizontal plane are equal, the drawing is *symmetrically dimetric*. The object revolves on a horizontal axis (fig. 3-3). A drawing is *unsymmetrically dimetric* if the top (or bottom) and one side are mirror images of each other. The object revolves on a vertical axis (fig. 3-4).

Dimetric drawings are useful for the same reasons that isometric ones are; in addition, they are capable of focusing attention on a specific side of the object.

Problem 21:
Symmetrically
dimetric cube

Using a pencil and grid paper, draw a vertical line. Make two similar angles on either side of the bottom of that line. Duplicate the angles at the top of the vertical line. Add the remaining lines, parallel to the existing lines, to form a cube. The angles can be at any degree. When they are at a 30-degree angle with the horizontal, the cube becomes isometric.

Problem 22:
Unsymmetrically
dimetric cube

Using a pencil and grid paper, draw one side of a cube composed of two parallel vertical lines and two parallel oblique (slanting) lines forming a second parallelogram. Add a mirror image second side to one of the oblique lines. Complete the cube with two lines, to form the third parallelogram.

Figures 3-3, 3-4

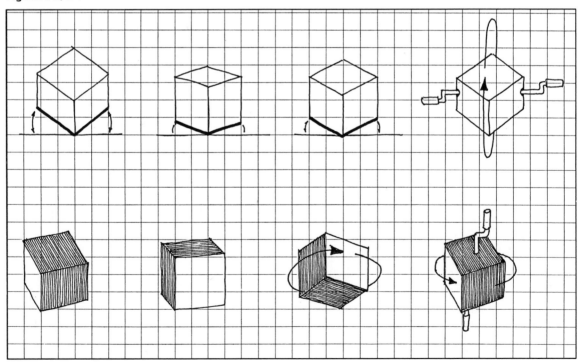

OBLIQUES

Oblique drawings are commonly used in architecture because they are easy to construct from a plan, a section, or an elevation. There are two kinds of obliques, plan obliques and elevation obliques.

A *plan oblique* begins by orienting a plan with one corner pointing down. The corner's angle with a horizontal is not important. In hard-line drawing, a 30- or 60-degree angle is almost always used, simply for convenience. A 45-degree angle is not as good, for reasons that will become clear. From each corner of the plan, lines are extended vertically a certain distance. Just as the plan is measurable in its two directions, so the vertical distance is measurable. When the vertical lines are connected at their tops, they will form a plan identical with the original (fig. 3-5).

If the angle of the plan is at 45 degrees to the horizontal, the vertical lines will fall on top of each other, creating confusion. Hence, any other angle is better than a 45-degree angle.

Two characteristics identify a plan oblique. The plan is always parallel to the pic-

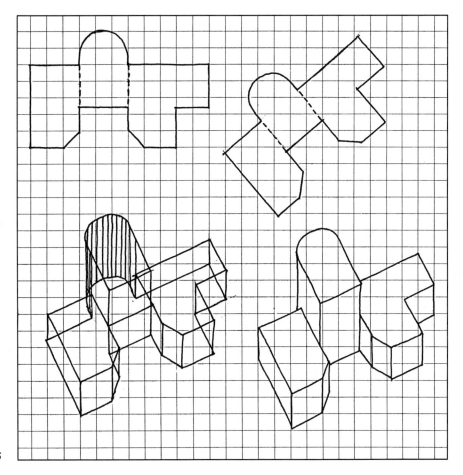

Figure 3-5

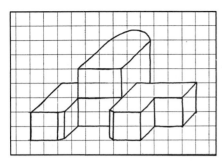

Figure 3-6

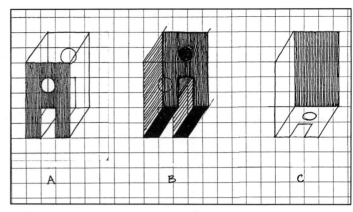

A   B   C

Figure 3-7

ture plane. And, no matter how high the structure is, the point of view always remains the same.

In drawing a plan oblique, it is important that the plan be rotated so that a corner is pointing down and the verticals *be* vertical. If the sight lines are simply drawn off to one side of the plan, an *elevation oblique* will surely ensue. It is an optical problem.

An *elevation oblique* starts with an elevation instead of a plan. Extend sight lines from each corner, going off at a convenient angle. When the ends of the lines are connected they will form a similar elevation (fig. 3-6).

In figure 3-7, A, B, and C all have the same rectangular profile. The orientation reflects the different projections. A is an elevation oblique; B is a plan oblique. C is another view, included to show how confusing things can become.

The plan oblique, figure 3-7B, should of course be turned so that a corner is pointing down. Not only will that keep it from automatically looking like an elevation oblique, but we tend to prefer seeing a structure with its sides vertical.

These days the word *axonometric*, or *axon*, is tossed around architectural schools like confetti. Almost always, the drawings referred to are plan obliques, not axonometrics.

Paraline drawings, like certain other nonperspective ways of seeing, can project mysterious unplumbed depths when they are turned into graphic images. As in the prints of M.C. Escher, it is sometimes hard to tell which end is up.

Problem 23:
Composition in
paraline using
letters

Use a pencil and grid paper. Using the letters of your name, all or in part, create in paraline a unified composition of monumental parts. Remember to consider your whole page as part of the composition—the image cannot be a tiny drawing on a large page. The letters may be joined together; they may overlap. Intersections may melt together. Your composition should have a message: not a literal one, but an emotional one. It could speak of autocracy, of dependency, perhaps of sublimation, but above all it should speak of unity. Figures 3-8, 3-9, and 3-10 are three outstanding student solutions to the problem.

Figure 3-8

**Problem 24:
Four plan
obliques**

This problem was devised to reinforce paraline concepts as well as to focus attention on the meshing of parts and the interaction of space and solids. Use a pencil and grid paper. A simple plan/footprint has been provided (fig. 3-11). Repeat this plan four times, raising a different superstructure on each, drawn in plan oblique. Each of the four units is to be seen from a different angle. The units must be composed so that the sheet is filled or so that it is clear that the whole page has been considered. Units may overlap or touch, and they do not necessarily have to be vertical. The completed composition should be a synthesis of disparate parts forming a coherent whole. (See figs. 3-12 and 3-13).

Figure 3-9

Figure 3-10

Figure 3-12

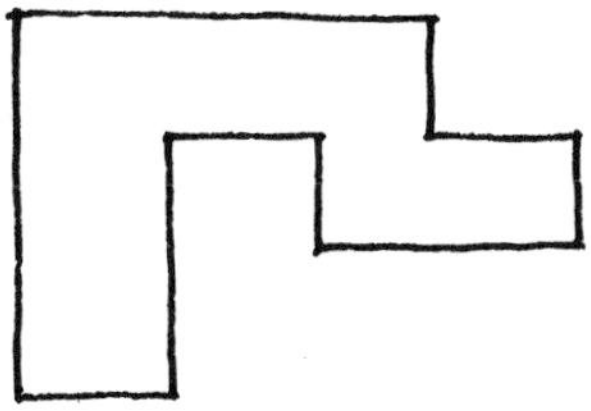

Figure 3-11

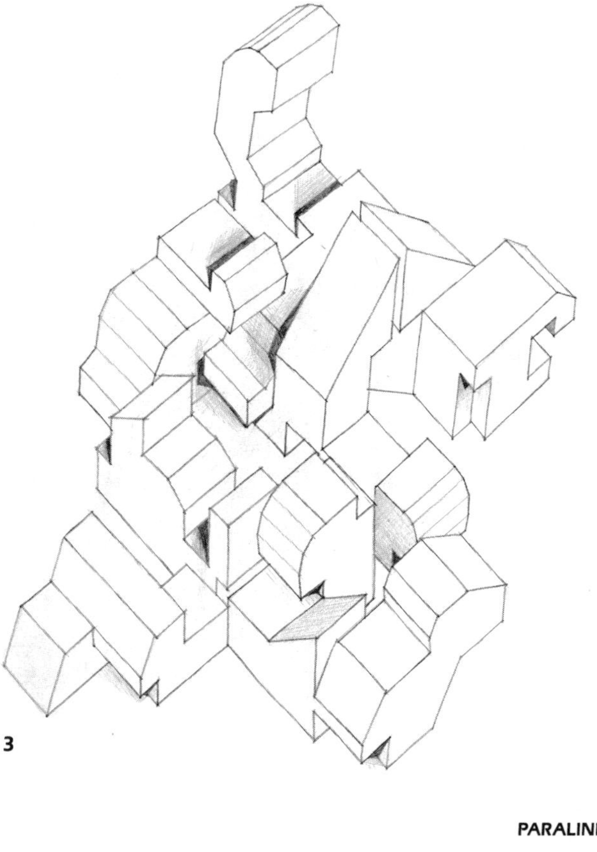

Figure 3-13

Problem 25:
Ten exercises in
descriptive
geometry

Culled from the annals of descriptive geometry are problems that force a student to try to see solutions in three dimensions, to visualize volumes and spaces, and to think logically, such as this problem. Use a pencil and grid paper. Figure 3-14 shows a set of simple shapes, in plan and in front and side elevation. Visualize and draw them in paraline—in other words, three sides are to be visible. (See fig. 3-15.)

For the student who cannot determine the proper configuration, the best approach is to start drawing the front bottom corner of a cube, onto which can be sketched the front and side elevations, trying to make them fit.

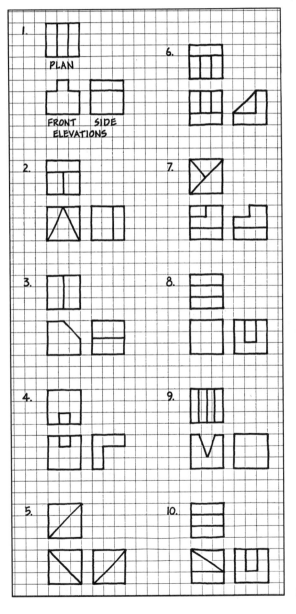

Figure 3-14

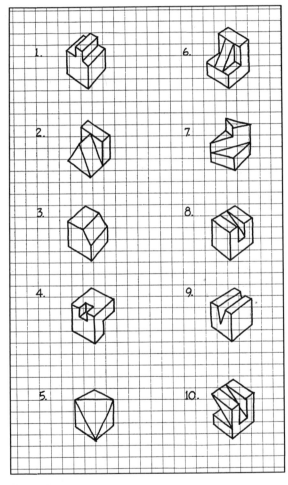

Figure 3-15

Problem 26:
Composition of
ten solids

Use a pencil and grid paper. The ten solids resulting from problem 25 are palpably buildable shapes. Create a composition by welding the shapes together into one piece of sculpture. Shading can be used to increase the feeling of solidity. (See figs. 3-16 and 3-17.)

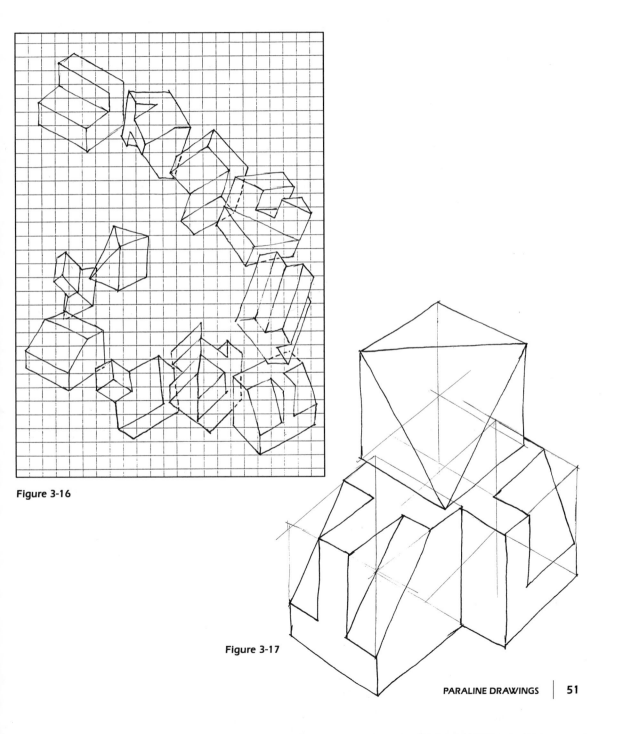

Figure 3-16

Figure 3-17

4.

Shade and Shadow

Shade is usually defined as an area or plane that is dark because it receives no light. A *shadow* is the image of that dark area or plane cast onto the ground or another object. Although experiments have shown that there is no difference between the value, or relative darkness, of shade and of shadow, conventionally shadows are represented as darker than shade.

Shadows breathe life into a drawing, giving it the chiaroscuro of the real world. (Chiaroscuro means the arrangement of light and dark areas.) In addition, they supply specific information about depth and contour.

When one is outside, drawing structures and landscapes, it is only necessary to copy the shadows and shades that one sees. Inside at the drawing board, shadows for these subjects have to be constructed or made up. We are interested only in shadows that can easily be constructed freehand. For these, just enough accuracy is needed to keep from spoiling the rendering. Though relatively few people know how to cast a shadow, the whole world knows when it is not right.

CASTING SHADOWS
IN ORTHOGRAPHIC PROJECTIONS

Casting shadows is an expression used to indicate that a formula has been involved in the drawing of the proper shadow. The easiest way to learn about shadow casting is to start with the orthographic projections. Why add shadows to an orthographic projection, which by definition has no depth indicators? Precisely because of the inherent lack of depth: shadows give the flat drawing an appearance of depth and, just as important, establish a relationship of depths.

Back in the studio, where there is no sun to serve as a guide, two decisions must be made. First, how high is the sun in the sky? This is the *sun angle*. Second, where is the sun in the sky? This is the *direction of the sun's rays*.

Unquestionably the easiest way to cast shadows from objects positioned orthographically to a base line is to assume the sun angle to be 45 degrees and the direction of the sun's rays also to be 45 degrees. The depth or distance of a shadow is related to the depth or height of the object casting the shadow and to the angle and direction of the light source. Therefore, if a 45-degree angle is used as both the direction and the angle of the sun, the width of the shadow in plan will be equal to the height of the plane casting it. Similarly, in elevation the depth of a shadow below an overhang will be the same as the width of the overhang.

In orthographic views, if the height of a wall is known or the width of an overhang is known, it is possible to plot the shadow on a parallel surface without having to use hard-line drawing instruments or a plan and elevations in conjunction. More complicated ways of representing shadows that cannot be accomplished freehand can be used, but they are beyond the scope of this book.

There is one cardinal rule that applies to all shadow casting: *lines cast parallel shadows on parallel surfaces.*

CASTING SHADOWS IN PLAN

The plan of a building is actually a horizontal section, generally taken about 4 or 5 feet above the ground. To cast the shadows from walls in plan, it is necessary first to decide the direction of the shadows in the drawing—up and to the right? Down and to the left? Down and right? The decision depends solely on the way the finished product will look on the page. Once this decision has been made, the location of the sun will be known, because the sun can be in only one particular position to produce shadows in the chosen direction. The sun's direction line is now added in the proper direction and extended until the perpendicular distance from the wall is the same as the wall's height (fig. 4-1).

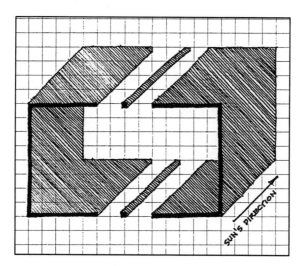

Figure 4-1

Problem 27:
Casting a
shadow from a
wall in plan

Use a pencil and grid paper. Assign a value of 2 feet to the grid squares. Draw, in plan a wall 20 feet long and 4 feet wide, situated horizontally. The wall is 6 feet high. Assume that the shadows will be cast up and to the right on the paper. Start the shadow from the lower right corner of the wall, and draw it at a 45-degree angle up and to the right, until the perpendicular distance from the side of the wall equals 6 feet. Draw a similar line from the top right corner of the wall until it also reaches a perpendicular distance from the side of the wall of 6 feet. Connect the two lines, noticing that the connecting line is parallel to the line that is casting it and that its vertical distance is 4 feet—the width of the wall. Draw a line from the top left corner of the wall, at a 45-degree angle, until its perpendicular distance from the top of the wall equals 6 feet. Connect the lines.

**Problem 28:
Casting a
shadow from a
wall in plan**

Use a pencil and grid paper. Draw, in plan, a wall 20 feet long and 6 feet wide, situated vertically. The wall is 10 feet high. Following the directions for problem 27, cast a shadow from the wall. (See fig. 4-2.)

**Problem 29:
Casting shadows
from walls of
different heights**

Use a pencil and grid paper. Draw a plan of shapes with different heights. Cast shadows at a 45-degree angle up and to the right, making the shadow widths reflect the differing heights of the parts of the structure. (See fig. 4-3.)

When the plan is on a sloping site and the top of the wall remains horizontal, the shadow will be progressively farther from the wall as the height of wall increases (fig. 4-4).

In plan, the sun's direction line is straight even if the shadow is falling across steps, slopes, tank traps, or other inclined ground.

Figure 4-2

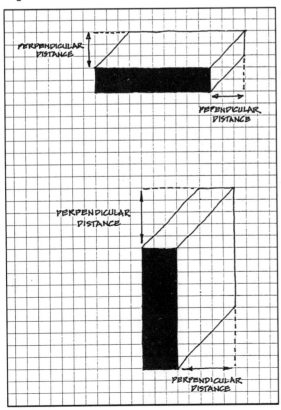

Figures 4-3, 4-4

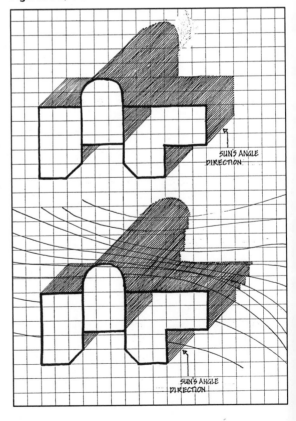

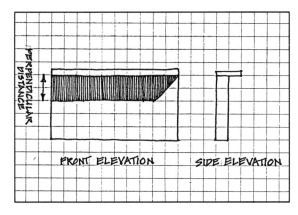

Figure 4-5

CASTING SHADOWS IN ELEVATION

Shadows in elevation are the same as shadows in plan except that the plane is vertical instead of horizontal. The measurement here is down rather than across, in order to find the depth of the overhang rather than the height of the wall. The depth of the shadow under the overhang will be the same as the width of the overhang. The diagonal line is the sun's angle line instead of the sun's direction line.

Problem 30:
Casting shadows
in elevation

Use a pencil and grid paper. Assign a value of 2 feet to the grid squares. Your drawing will represent the wall of a building in elevation. It will be 10 feet high, 20 feet wide, and 2 feet thick. It will have a roof overhang that is 1 foot thick and projects forward 4 feet.

Cast the shadow down and to the left. The shadow line will begin at the upper right corner of the *bottom* of the overhang, because that is the edge that is casting the shadow. Draw the line down and to the left at a 45-degree angle until the perpendicular distance from the overhang is equivalent to 4 feet. The line will now run parallel to the edge of the overhang, because lines cast parallel shadows on parallel surfaces. (See fig. 4-5.)

Problem 31:
Casting shadows
in elevation

Use a pencil and grid paper. Assign a value of 2 feet to the grid squares. This drawing will represent the wall of a building in elevation. It will be 14 feet wide and 12 feet tall and will have a roof overhang 1 foot thick that will extend forward 4 feet. It will have a 6- by 6-foot window recess 6 feet from the left side and 4 feet above the ground. The recess will be 1 foot deep.

Start by casting the shadow from the overhang. It will begin at the upper right corner at the bottom edge of the overhang. Draw the shadow line down at an angle of 45 degrees until the perpendicular distance from the overhang is 4 feet. The line will now run left, parallel to the roof overhang.

Now consider what will happen inside the window recess. Since the recess is 1 foot deep, the shadow inside the recess will be 1 foot lower than the shadow on the wall. The right side of the recess will be casting a shadow too, so add a 1-foot shadow to the right-hand side of the recess.

The use of shadows on elevations is common. On a site plan, they are used by landscape architects to indicate relative heights of trees, buildings, steps, and walls. They are rarely included in section drawings.

SHADOWS ON STEPS IN PLAN AND ELEVATION

Steps appear somewhere on almost all elevations and site plans. The construction of shadows on steps, even in the orthographic views, usually goes beyond the limits of easy freehand drawing. It is enough to know the pattern that they make, so that they will look accurate when sketched.

Steps in the sun almost always have an accompanying wall or railing that is either horizontal to the ground plane or that follows the angle of the steps. In plan and elevation they follow a common scheme.

Shadows from a wall whose top is horizontal to the steps will abide by the 45-degree-angle rule: the width of the shadow is equivalent to the height of the wall casting it. Therefore the shadows on the steps bounce down according to the wall's height until they reach the sun's direction line. The direction line attaches to the corner that casts it.

A paraline drawing, like that in figure 4-6, shows what is really happening in the plan and elevation diagrams. In elevation the sun's angle line starts down until it meets the width marks as projected down from the plan above.

In plan *and* elevation, shadows from a wall (or railing) that follow the angle of the steps will remain the same width on all the steps because, of course, the top of the wall or railing is continuously the same height above the steps. The angle of the shadow back to the wall requires hard-line construction. A paraline drawing, as in figure 4-7, shows what is really happening in the plan and elevation diagrams: a zig-zag shadow line has resulted.

Figure 4-6

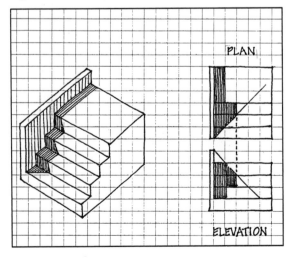

Figure 4-7

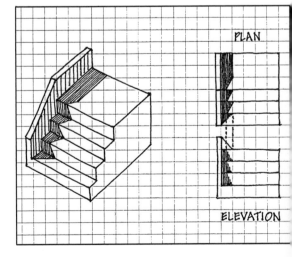

SHADOWS IN PARALINE

Shadow casting can become awesomely complicated when dealing with shadows from inclined planes falling on other inclined planes. One is reduced to constructing these by using a plan and an elevation, sometimes even two elevations. Our mission here is not to delve into such complexities but to furnish the novice artist with guidelines that will be useful in the most commonly encountered situations. All of the shadows described here can be drawn freehand, with the help of gridded paper.

Paraline drawings are not orthographic and therefore the simple way of casting shadows in plan and elevation no longer holds. Shadows in paraline involve a method that will cover all sorts of three-dimensional drawings, including, eventually, perspective.

Whenever possible, cast shadows to the right (or left) and back (up, on the page), because this means that the light is hitting the object from the front. Back-lighting may be interesting in photography but is not very descriptive in a drawing.

Most of the time a sun direction that is horizontal to the picture plane will provide a pleasing result and also be easy to control. Only the angle of the sun is left to determine. The following instructions apply to shadows that have a direction that is horizontal to the picture plane.

The position of shadows will be found by plotting the points that cast the shadows. The points will generally be the ends of the lines or the planes that are in shade.

**Problem 32:
Shadows from a
paraline box**

Use a pencil and grid paper. Draw a box in paraline—that is, a three-sided view with all pairs of sides parallel. Shade one side. The edges that will cast the shadows are the ones that form the boundary between the light and the dark. Draw a right triangle in which the vertical will be the edge of the plane in shade, the horizontal will be the direction of the sun's rays, and the hypotenuse will be the angle of the sun's rays (fig. 4-8). This will be called a directional triangle.

The shadow of point A will be at point B, the intersection of the horizontal and the oblique lines. Construct a similar triangle from the next point on the object. In the case of points on the back side of the object, the object will need to be drawn in wire frame (transparent) in order to locate the points. Continue until all points are accounted for, and then join them with a line (fig. 4-9). Shade the shadow.

Notice that there are just two kinds of shadow lines here: those cast by vertical edges and those cast by horizontal edges. Horizontal lines cast shadows that run along the ground in a parallel fashion, while vertical lines cast shadows that follow the direction of the sun's rays. This follows the rule that a shadow casts a parallel line on a parallel plane, which is why, in figure 4-10, lines 1 and 2 are parallel and lines 3 and 4 are parallel.

**Problem 33:
Shadows from a
paraline box**

Use pencil and grid paper. Draw several boxes in paraline. Cast shadows from them, using different sun angles.

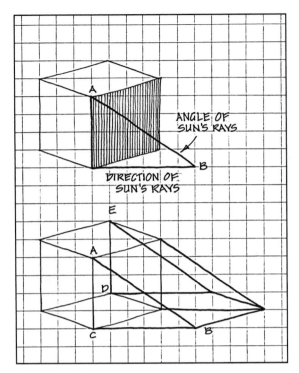

Figures 4-8, 4-9

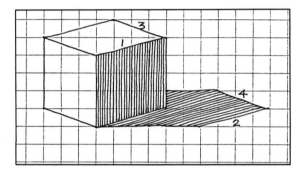

Figure 4-10

Besides the shadows from rectilinear structures, it is necessary to know several other indigestible but ubiquitous shadow effects: on vertical surfaces, under overhangs, and on stairs.

In many of these cases it is not convenient or reasonable to use a shadow whose direction is horizontal. When the direction of the sun's rays is other than horizontal, it is helpful to draw a small triangle to illustrate the direction and the angle, as in figure 4-11.

SHADOWS ON VERTICAL SURFACES

To clarify what is happening to the shadow as the sun's direction and angle change, it is helpful to follow the movement of the shadow of the top corner of the wall. In figure 4-12 the shadow of point A is point B. If point B stays on the ground plane, the shadow line will head for point C when it reaches the vertical plane. If the shadow line reaches the vertical plane before getting to point B, as in figure 4-13, then the shadow line will rise vertically on the vertical plane until it reaches the line from point A to point B, then head for point C.

If the walls are back-lit, the shadows will be coming toward the viewer. The system remains the same. A directional triangle will be drawn from the front side of each wall and the points joined by lines parallel to the tops of the walls (fig. 4-14).

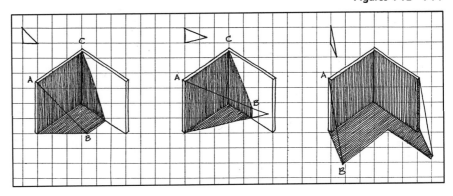

Figure 4-11

Figures 4-12 – 4-14

Problem 34:
Casting shadows on a vertical surface

Use pencil and grid paper. Draw two walls at a right angle to each other in paraline. Orient them so as to be looking into the corner. Cast a shadow from the left wall toward the right at an angle of about 10 degrees from the horizontal. This is the sun's direction line. Make it a bit longer than the vertical. The direction line and the vertical are two sides of the directional triangle. Add the third side. Draw the line that is the shadow of the horizontal top of the wall. It will be parallel to the top of the wall and will continue until it reaches the bottom of the adjoining wall. There it will go straight to the top corner, joining the point that is casting the shadow.

Problem 35:
Casting shadows on a vertical surface

Use a pencil and grid paper. Draw two walls at a right angle to each other in paraline. Orient them so as to be looking into the corner. Cast a shadow from the left wall toward the right at an angle of about 45 degrees from the horizontal. Make this direction line long enough to extend into the adjoining wall. Add the third line of the directional triangle. The shadow line will extend along the direction line until it reaches the base of the adjoining wall, where it will rise vertically until it reaches the sun's angle line. Then it will go straight to the top corner, joining the point that is casting the shadow.

Problem 36:
Casting shadows toward the viewer

Use a pencil and grid paper. Draw two adjoining walls as in problems 34 and 35. Draw identical directional triangles off the ends of the walls. The direction line should be about 85 degrees below the horizontal, of any length. Complete the triangles. Connect the points with lines parallel to the tops of the walls.

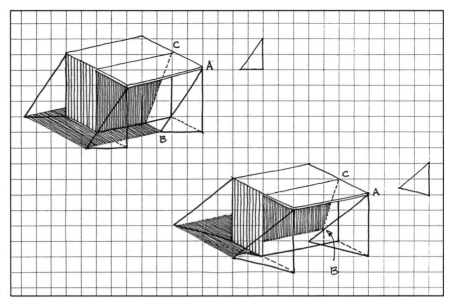

Figures 4-15, 4-16

SHADOWS UNDER OVERHANGS

Shadows under overhangs, as in figure 4-15, slant down the vertical surface (from point C) following the angle of the sun until they meet the hypotenuse of the directional triangle (point B), and then they continue parallel to the overhang edge. If the shadow is so deep that it reaches the ground, as in figure 4-16, the line must join the shadow of the point cast by the far edge of the overhang (at point B).

Problem 37:
Casting shadows
from overhangs

Use a pencil and grid paper. Draw a box in paraline, and cap it with an overhang. Draw a directional triangle from the outside corner of the overhang. Make the sun's direction a horizontal line, keeping the distance short enough that the shadow stays on the ground. Complete the triangle. The point of the triangle is the shadow of the corner of the overhang. The shadow will travel parallel to the side edge of the overhang until it reaches the vertical wall. There it will go straight home to the juncture of the overhang and the wall.

Problem 38:
Casting shadows
from overhangs

Use a pencil and grid paper. Draw a box in paraline, and cap it with an overhang. Draw a directional triangle from the outside corner of the overhang. Make the sun's direction at an angle of about 30 degrees from the horizontal, and continue the line far enough so that the point of the triangle falls within the vertical wall. Take a vertical line from the intersection of the triangle with the wall until it meets the hypotenuse of the triangle. That is the shadow of the outside corner of the overhang. The shadow line will go straight from that point to the juncture of the overhang with the wall.

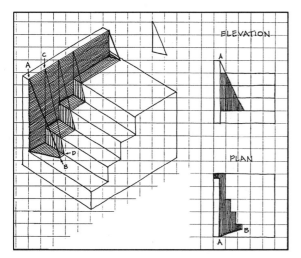

Figure 4-17

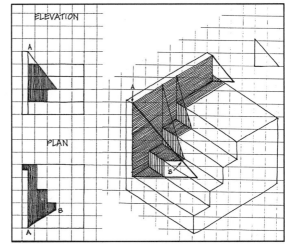

Figure 4-18

SHADOWS ON STEPS

Shadows on steps are just a series of shadows on vertical surfaces. The same directional triangle procedure is used to calculate the direction and angle of the sun's rays, as in figure 4-17. When the length of the shadow is short enough that point B falls on the first tread, the line on each succeeding tread is parallel to the wall casting it. Its distance from the wall decreases as the wall becomes shorter. The shadow line on the riser is determined as follows: a vertical is drawn from the corner of the riser where it meets the wall, taken to the top of the wall (point C), and using the directional triangle, returned to point D, to form the line of the shadow. When the shadow is long, point B will have moved up a step or two, as in figures 4-18 and 4-19. The shadow line on the riser will be vertical until point B is reached. After that, the shadow is drawn using the method for a short shadow. The plan and elevation are included with figures 4-17, 4-18, and 4-19 to show the movement of point B.

When the height of the stair wall follows the slope of the steps, the width of the shadow stays the same because the height of the wall remains the same distance above the steps (fig. 4-20).

Figure 4-21 shows stairs that have a railing instead of a wall. The railing follows the edge of the shadow.

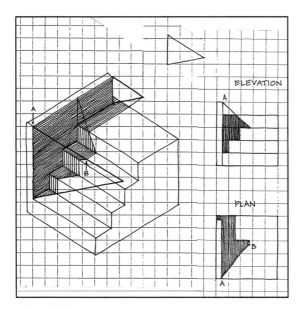

Figure 4-19

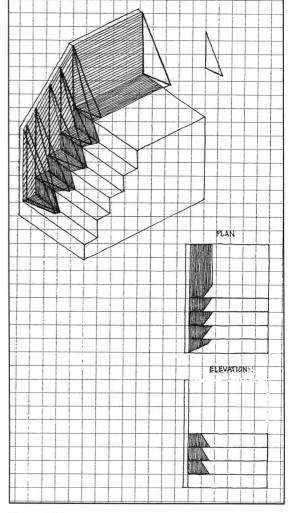

Figure 4-20

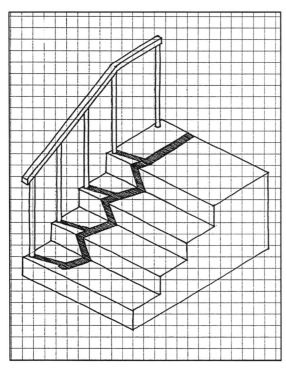

Figure 4-21

Problem 39:
Casting shadows
on steps

Use a pencil and grid paper. Draw a flight of steps in paraline that has a wall on one side whose top is parallel to the top of the steps.

Construct a directional triangle from the vertical front of the wall so that its point falls on the tread of the first step. From that point the line will run parallel with the top of the wall until it hits the vertical riser. The shadow line on the riser is found by taking a vertical from the corner of the riser where it meets the wall, up to the top of the wall, and then down until it meets the shadow line. Again the shadow line on the tread will be parallel with the top of the wall. Find the shadow line on the riser in the same way. Continue until reaching the top step.

Problem 40:
Casting shadows
on steps

Use a pencil and grid paper. Draw a set of steps in paraline that has a wall on one side whose top is parallel to the top of the steps.

Construct a directional triangle from the vertical front of the wall so that its point falls on the second step. When the direction line meets the riser, the shadow line will be vertical because it is parallel to the vertical of the wall. On the tread of the second step, the shadow line is parallel to its original direction until it meets the hypotenuse of the directional triangle. That point is the shadow of the top corner of the wall on the step. Continue as in the previous problem.

Problem 41:
Casting shadows
on steps

Use a pencil and grid paper. This is the most complicated freehand shadow problem included here. Remember that all you are doing is finding the shadows of points and then connecting them.

Draw a set of steps in paraline that has a wall on one side that slants at the same degree as the incline of the steps.

Construct a directional triangle from the vertical front of the wall so that its point falls on the first tread. Construct a second triangle parallel to the first so that its point falls just at the vertical of the second step. Connecting these two gives the shadow line from the top of the sloping wall onto the tread. Find the shadow line on the riser using the method described in problem 39. On each succeeding step, only one directional triangle will be needed, because you already have the first point of the shadow line.

SHADOWS IN PERSPECTIVE

There is no difference between shadows in perspective and shadows in paraline, except that in perspective parallel lines converge toward a vanishing point. If one is comfortable with perspective, casting shadows therein will pose no problems.

SHADOWS OUTDOORS

It is easy to forget, when drawing the outside world, that the sun's angle in the sky changes with dismaying speed. If the shadows on a building or in a landscape are particularly effective at one moment, that is the moment to proceed right through the drawing, lightly penciling in all the shadows. Then there is safety from time and clouds.

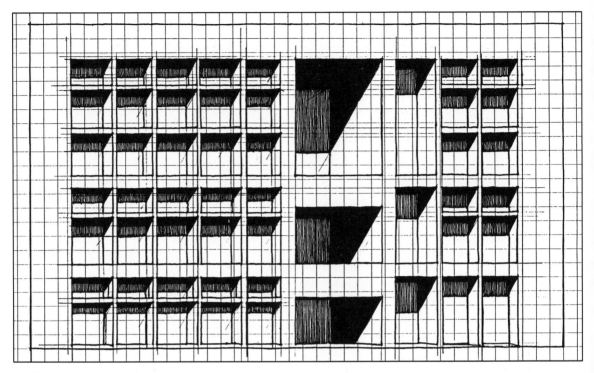

Figure 4-22

Make life easy for yourself when drawing outdoors. Generally assume that there will be a shadow under every overhang. Make the shadow lower where the overhangs are deeper. Glance at the sun's angle where it shows clearly, and use that angle for every edge that is parallel. Figure 4-22 is a student drawing of a facade showing the sun's angle and the depth of overhang. The rules of thumb for representing shadows in freehand drawing outdoors are:

- Be sure that the angle of the sun's rays is identical on all parallel surfaces.
- Make the depth of the shadow relate to the depth of the overhang.

5.

Perspective

The natural step beyond paraline is perspective, which is another kind of drawing in three dimensions, but one that removes the distortion and allows the world to come alive in its true form.

Those of us who are sighted interpret the world as having depth. We base this conclusion on five observable characteristics:

- Overlap: some objects appear to be behind others
- Diminution: objects appear to become smaller as they move farther away
- Value: objects close up appear to be darker and brighter than those far away
- Foreshortening: lines parallel to the line of sight of the observer appear to become shorter as they are rotated away from the observer
- Convergence: lines perpendicular to the line of sight of the observer appear to converge as they move farther away

All of these characteristics are part of drawing in perspective, part of the effort to make drawings look real.

Just as it is easy to superimpose a grid on a two-dimensional view to make it easier to draw, so it is easy to think about real-world volumes in space and to visualize them as relating to a three-dimensional grid. Grids are enormously flexible and can be adapted to fit over and bring order to everything we see and most of what we experience.

Movement, for example, can be understood as a set of serial views in a grid, each one advancing slightly in the direction of completion. Time-lapse photographs of flowers opening or buildings being built are space-time grids. They reduce action or growth to understandable units.

ONE-POINT PERSPECTIVE AND A GRID

One-point perspective is easy to grasp. Everytime we look straight across a room or look ahead as we drive down the city street, we are in a one-point-perspective time warp. If the road were to go on forever, the way it sometimes seems to do in Kansas,

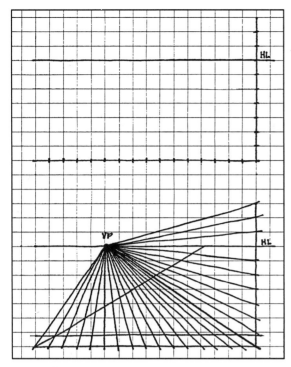

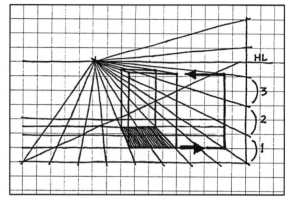

Figures 5-1, 5-2   Figure 5-3

without turning and without hills intervening, and if our eyes were good enough, the sides of the road would appear to get closer and closer together until vanishing at a spot on the horizon exactly level with our eye. Moreover, if we were to sit on the ground or perch atop a ladder, that vanishing point would still be on the horizon, perpendicular to our eye, dead ahead. We take our vanishing point with us.

Looking across a room is the same as looking down the road, if we could enclose it in a box.

Constructing a one-point-perspective grid is an easy introduction to this useful tool.

Problem 42:
One-point-
perspective grid

Use a pencil and grid paper. Draw a horizontal and a vertical axis. Tick them off in even increments. Draw a horizon line (HL) at some convenient height, as in figure 5-1. The convention is to set the horizon line at 5 feet, to approximate the eye level of a standing person, but in this case a 5-foot eye level would make the grid too dense, so put it at 7 feet. Put a vanishing point (VP) anywhere along the horizon line, and from it draw a line through each tick mark on each axis.

Now comes the step that marks the difference between freehand drawing and hard-line drawing (hard-line drawing presupposes the use of T square or parallel bar and triangle). Instead of locating the first horizontal line of the grid by a complicated system of measurements and arcs, simply draw a horizontal line above the horizontal axis to form polygons that look as if they are squares in perspective. The horizontal unit length will be a bit longer than the unit length extending to the vanishing point because lines extending to the vanishing point appear to shorten. Draw a diagonal from the bottom left corner of the leftmost polygon through its upper right corner, then extend it to the horizon (fig. 5-2). Each intersection of the diagonal with a line to the vanishing point marks the position of the next horizontal.

Objects or structures may be located easily on a grid by first positioning the footprint of the object on the horizontal grid and then raising it vertically the proper distance.

Problem 43:
Locating a box
on a grid

Use a pencil and grid paper. Draw a one-point-perspective grid. Place a 2- by 2- by 3-unit box on the grid by first drawing the footprint of the 2 by 2 box somewhere on the grid. Find the proper 3-unit height by extending a line from the front of the box horizontally over to the vertical axis. Rise to the proper height of 3 units, then bring the line back, horizontally, to the box. This is the height of the box. The top sides of the box are drawn to converge toward the vanishing point. (See fig. 5-3.)

The density of the grid increases very quickly. It is not possible to draw or to distinguish horizontal lines all the way back to the vanishing point. Raising the eye level allows a deeper view, as a comparison of figures 5-4 and 5-5 demonstrates.

Perspective as a tool is mainly concerned with objects or structures that have a number of parallel sides. One does not think about drawing a tree or a person in perspective. But perspective lines are frequently used to find the height of a person or tree, which is then simply drawn in the usual manner. A perspective grid is almost essential for calculating how something that has an irregular outline will appear on a wall or floor, for example, a strangely shaped wall hanging, a modernistic area rug, or a pond or planting bed.

Figures 5-4, 5-5

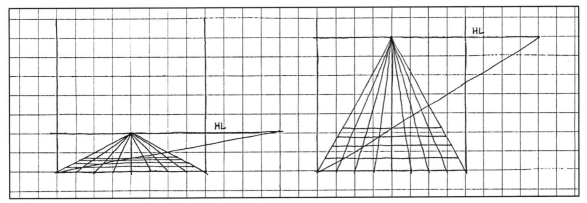

Problem 44:
Perspective of an
irregular shape

Use a pencil and grid paper. Draw an irregular shape. Since it is drawn on gridded paper, it is already gridded, but it is probably more practical to use only every other grid line. Heavy up the grid lines so you can see them better.

Construct a one-point-perspective grid. Transfer the irregular shape to the one-point-perspective grid by noting where the irregular line enters and leaves each square. (See figs. 5-6 and 5-7.)

INTERIOR ONE-POINT PERSPECTIVE

One-point perspective is used frequently in interiors. A quickly sketched grid can be the base for a realistic interior complete with rises in level, furniture, scale figures, and other elements.

Problem 45:
Interior
one-point-
perspective
drawing

Use a pencil and grid paper. Assign a value to the grid squares of 1 foot. Draw the back wall of a room, a simple rectangle that is 15 feet long and 8 feet high. Tick off 1-foot increments along one side and the base of the wall.

To cut down on the blizzard of lines that a grid is wont to produce, you will construct only those that are needed.

Draw a horizon line at 5 feet and a vanishing point anywhere on the horizon line. From the vanishing point, extend lines an arbitrary distance through the back corner of the wall, to begin forming the sides, floor, and ceiling of your interior space. Extend the ground line (GL), ticking off a distance equal to the depth you want your space to be, say 6 feet. On the same side, extend the horizon line (HL) to a distance somewhat greater than the ground line (GL), and mark an exterior vanishing point (EVP). Draw a line from this point through the 6-foot measuring mark on the ground line until it reaches the line coming from the vanishing point. A horizontal line from this point establishes the depth of the space at 6 feet. Complete the rectangle started by the horizontal 6-foot line. (See fig. 5-8.)

Problem 46:
Interior
one-point-
perspective
drawing

Use a pencil and grid paper. Construct a one-point-perspective interior, using back-wall dimensions of 15 by 8 feet. Give the room a depth of 6 feet, following the instructions for problem 45.

Take a line from the exterior vanishing point through the opposite lower corner of the back-wall rectangle to establish a grid that appears to be behind the picture plane—as though you were gazing out through a glass wall onto a patio, for instance (fig. 5-9).

Draw a low wall around the outdoor patio, making sure all lines extend to the appropriate vanishing points.

In freehand drawing the position of the exterior vanishing point is arbitrary. As it is pulled farther away from the rectangle, the apparent depth of the room becomes shallower. (In hard-line drawing the position of the vanishing point is set by the station point of the observer as it is found in the plan.)

The clarity of the floor grid depends on the eye level. As it is raised, the compacting of the horizontal lines becomes less. However, the distortion in the foreground becomes greater. A delicate balance is needed.

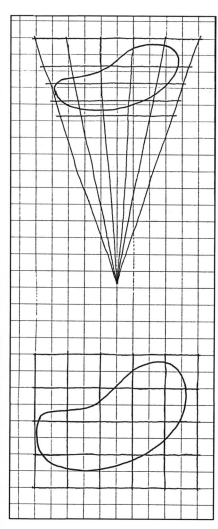

Figures 5-6, 5-7

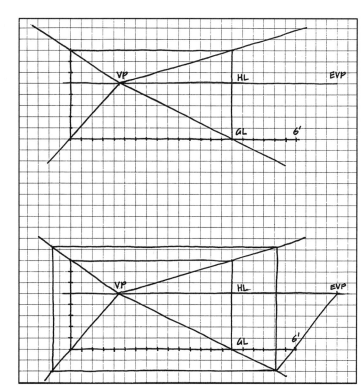

Figure 5-8

Figure 5-9

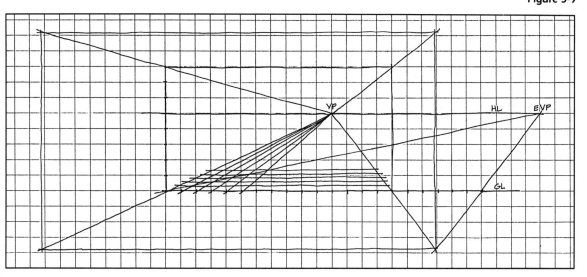

EXTERIOR ONE-POINT PERSPECTIVE

Exterior one-point perspective involves a much larger scale, since it is commonly used for street scenes. From an eye level of 5 feet, the near buildings will go off the top of the page. A higher eye level allows more of the near buildings to show but decreases the humanness of the scene. Figures are essential for scale, as illustrated in figure 5-10.

No matter how quickly a sketch is being drawn and no matter if it is being drawn from life or if it is being created from the imagination, a vanishing point should be established and from it the heights of people, cars, windows, and other important divisions should be established.

Problem 47: Exterior one-point-perspective drawing

Use pencil and grid paper. Set up a simple one-point-perspective grid by drawing a horizontal and a vertical axis and ticking them off. Add a horizon line at 10 feet, and put a vanishing point close to the middle. Draw an array of lines from the vanishing point to the ticks on the axes within which to create a city street scene with buildings of varied heights. Setbacks on the buildings are easily made. Include a cross street and sidewalks.

Figure 5-10

TWO-POINT PERSPECTIVE AND A GRID

A mastery of two-point perspective is perhaps the most valuable drawing skill of any for architects, since the drawings made with it are the ones people want to see. It provides the most realistic view. It corresponds to the way we see the world. Two-point-perspective drawings sell ideas. Learn to draw them quickly and accurately.

Two-point perspective is used whenever two sides of a rectangular object—or, any object that has primarily parallel sides—can be seen. Two-point perspective means that two vanishing points are used, one for each side of the object being depicted.

Drawing boxes is a good introduction to two-point perspective because it is simple enough to allow the system to be grasped quickly. Once the principle is understood, it is easily adapted to complex structures.

Problem 48: Two-point perspective of a box on the eye level

Use a pencil and grid paper. Draw a vertical line representing the near corner of a box and draw a horizontal line that shall be the horizon line. (Be aware that the terms *eye level* and *horizon line* are synonymous.) Draw your line so that it goes through the box, thus making your box *on* the eye level.

To say that an object is on the eye level is confusing, since it can be construed in several different ways. It can mean that the box is sitting on the horizon line. It can mean that the box is hanging from the horizon line. Or it can mean that the horizon line goes through the box. If the term is not clarified, you may take your choice of interpretations.

The vertical line that is the front corner of the box acts as the vertical measure. It can be ticked off in equal increments, allowing the horizon line to go through it at the desired height.

Add a vanishing point on the horizon line far to the right and another one far to the left. Connect the points to the top and bottom of the vertical line to form the top and bottom of the box. All that remains is to draw two vertical lines for the back ends of the box. In freehand perspective the lines forming the back sides of the box are eyeballed. Put them where they make the box look right. (See fig. 5-11.)

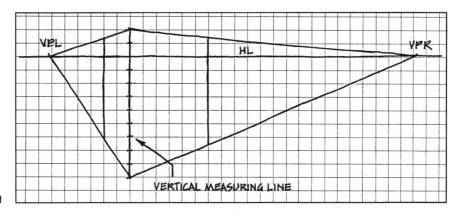

Figure 5-11

Problem 49:
Two-point
perspective of a
box above the
eye level

Use a pencil and grid paper. Draw a vertical line representing the near corner of the box. If the corner edge of the box is placed below the horizon line, the box will be below the eye level. If the corner edge of the box is placed above the horizon line, the box will be above the eye level. Draw your horizon line below the vertical line. Put one vanishing point far to the right on the horizon line and another vanishing point far to the left on the horizon line. Connect the top and bottom of the vertical line to the vanishing points on each side. Eyeball the back sides of the box. Now complete the bottom of the box by taking lines from the back sides to the appropriate vanishing points.

Problem 50:
Two-point
perspective of a
box below the
eye level

Use a pencil and grid paper. Draw a vertical for the near corner of a box. Add a horizon line above the vertical. Add a vanishing point far to the right on the horizon line and one far to the left. Connect the top and bottom of the vertical line to the vanishing points on either side. Eyeball the back sides of the box. Complete the top of the box by taking lines from the back sides to the appropriate vanishing points.

Problem 51:
Composition of
nine boxes

Use a pencil and grid paper. Draw nine boxes. Three boxes should be in one-point perspective: one on the eye level, one above the eye level, and one below the eye level. Three boxes should be in two-point perspective, viewed as though they were off to your right: one on the eye level, one above the eye level, one below the eye level. Three boxes should be in two-point perspective, viewed as though they were off to your left, again on, above, and below eye level. The boxes can be any size: they can overlap, they can all share two vanishing points, or there can be many vanishing points. All of the construction lines are to be shown; they may become an active part of the composition or they can be relegated to the background. You may use shading if you wish; you may vary the weight of the lines.

Most important is that an interesting composition be created. The composition must take the whole page into consideration. Little bitty boxes in the middle of the page will not do. (See fig. 5-12.)

Problem 52:
Nine-box
composition in
ink

Use pencil, pen, and tracing paper or vellum. Trace your completed nine-box composition from problem 51 onto a piece of tracing paper, using a pencil and drawing very lightly. If you care to make some small changes to improve the image, do so. You may leave out the construction lines if you feel they do not add anything. Render the composition in ink, using shading where you think it will improve the looks. Solid black is acceptable. The new composition should stand on its own, without regard to the first pencil drawing.

Problem 52 particularly calls for a critique because it is a composition in which many different requirements had to be considered. All of them must be addressed and the results evaluated. First, of course, the perspective of the boxes must be correct. Then lines need to be straight, some sort of a pattern should be evident, and the grouping of shapes and the play of values should work together to elicit a positive response.

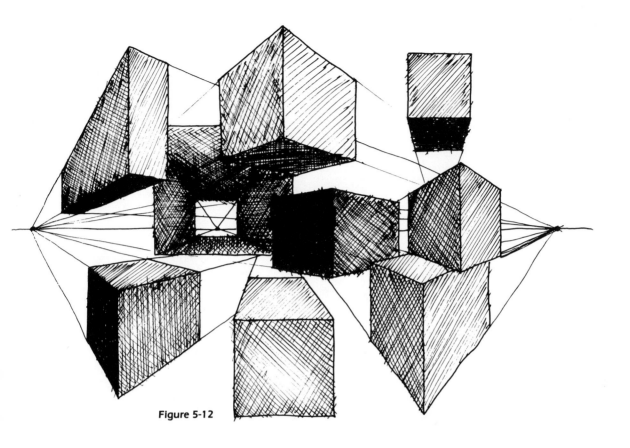

Figure 5-12

If the student has realized that the boxes look the same if they are viewed off to the right or off to the left, he or she is clear eyed and bushy tailed.

DISTORTION

In a two-point-perspective drawing, at least one of the vanishing points must be as far away as the paper will allow, or too much distortion will result.

Perspective is a mechanical means of drawing something so that it looks "right." It will only look right if the object being drawn is fairly close to being perpendicular to the eye. When objects move off to the right or the left, or far up or far down, the canons that govern perspective go awry; truth is no longer what it seems.

The rule of geometry that governs distortion says that if the angle of the near corner of the object is less than 45 degrees, the distortion will be unacceptable. In practice this means that, if the vanishing points are too close together, the result will look as though an amateur had drawn it, even though the rules of perspective have been followed.

At least one vanishing point should be at the far edge of the paper, or better yet off the paper and onto the table somewhere (fig. 5-13).

Figure 5-14 demonstrates that as one vanishing point moves farther away the other one moves closer in.

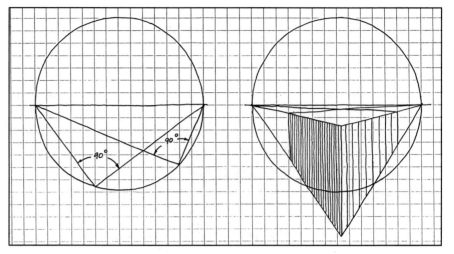

Figure 5-13

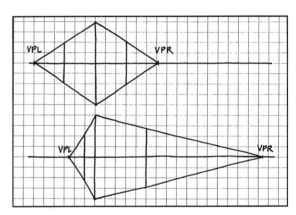

Figure 5-14

USING DIAGONALS TO PRODUCE EQUAL DIVISIONS

To draw a structure with many equal segments, such as bays, a method based on the division of a polygon by crossing its diagonals is used. It will work for any set of equal divisions: telephone poles, fence posts, rows of cars, city blocks. The system is described in problem 53.

**Problem 53:
Division of space
with the
diagonal method**

Use a pencil and grid paper. Draw a box in two-point perspective. Extend the top and bottom horizontals of each side of the box to their respective vanishing points (forming lines B and C, as in fig. 5-15). Find the center of one side of the box by crossing the diagonals. From the intersection of the diagonals, draw a line to the vanishing point. Extend a line from either the top or bottom near corner of the side of the box through the intersection of the line you just drew and the far side of the box (point A) until it meets either line B or C. Draw a vertical at that spot. Continue until you have at least four divisions. The system can be repeated as often as necessary and can be used in any direction and on any plane.

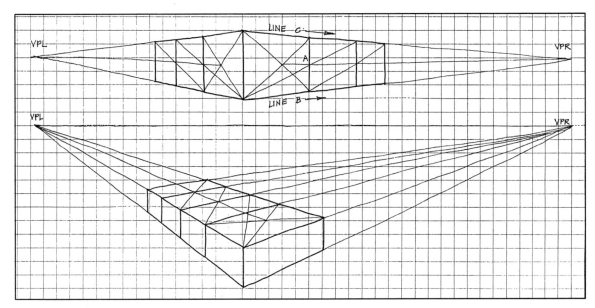

Figures 5-15, 5-16

Problem 54:
Two-point-
perspective grid

Did you realize that the tops of a series of boxes in two-point perspective (fig. 5-16) form a two-point-perspective grid? Use a pencil and grid paper. Draw a horizon line, and add two vanishing points to it, far apart. Put a point below the horizon line and extend a line to it from each vanishing point.

The next step involves estimation, marking the difference between freehand and hard-line drawing. Draw two more lines from the vanishing points so that their intersection, combined with the existing intersection, forms a polygon that looks like it is a square in perspective (fig. 5-17). Using the diagonal method, flesh out a two-point-perspective grid.

This grid, used in conjunction with a vertical measure, will give you a three-dimensional grid into which you can plug three-dimensional units (fig. 5-18).

GABLES IN TWO-POINT PERSPECTIVE

Drawing gable ends on a building also involves the use of crossed diagonals. A gable is the vertical triangular area, under the ridge and above the eaves.

Problem 55:
A double-pitched
roof in two-point
perspective

Use a pencil and grid paper. Draw a rectangular box in two-point perspective with an eye level at 5 feet. Find the optical center of one side of the box by crossing the diagonals of the polygon. Draw a vertical line through the crossing, as high as you want the gable of the roof to be. This will be the ridge of the roof. Draw lines from the ridge down to the upper corners of the side of the box. The ridge line will go to the appropriate vanishing point.

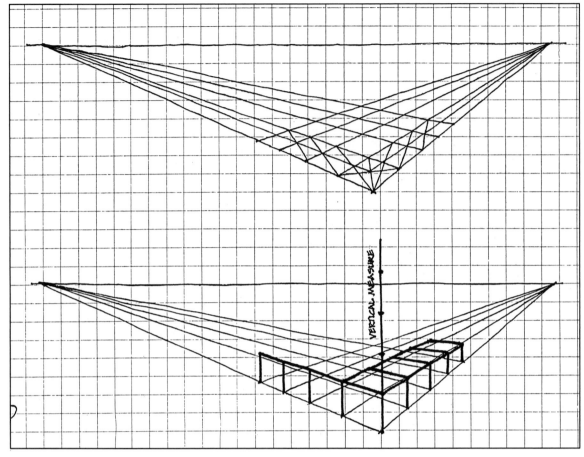

Figures 5-17, 5-18

Figure 5-19

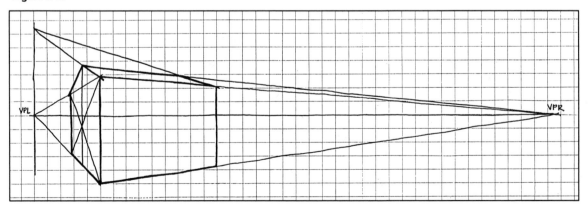

The far-end gable line can be tackled in two ways. The quick and easy way is to say that the gable line is parallel to the front gable line, plus a bit more. The more time-consuming way is to extend the front gable line until it meets a line taken vertically from its vanishing point. Draw the back gable line to that intersection (fig. 5-19).

INTERIOR TWO-POINT PERSPECTIVE

An interior view changes from one-point perspective to two-point perspective when one gazes into a corner instead of straight on. Interior two-points are perhaps more interesting views than one-points because, as always, horizontal and vertical lines have less pep than obliques.

Problem 56:
Interior
two-point
perspective

Use a pencil and grid paper. Draw a vertical line to form the corner that you are looking into. Tick it off for use as a vertical measure. Draw a horizon line at the chosen height. From the top and bottom of the vertical line draw a line to vanishing points (on the horizon of course), right and left. Make one of the vanishing points far away and the other near. Extend the lines from the vanishing points past the vertical and out into space (fig. 5-20).

The next step is the one in which a judgment call is made, in the true spirit of freehand drawing. Estimate a square in perspective on the right side of the vertical and one on the left. One will be wider than the other because it is being seen with less perspective. Using the diagonal method, construct squares as far in either direc-

Figure 5-20

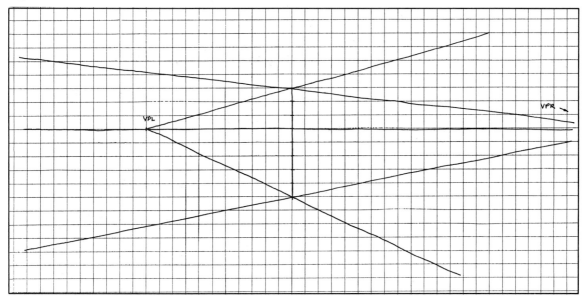

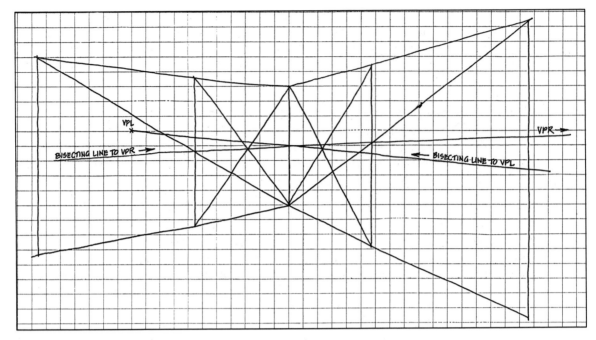

Figure 5-21

tion as you need them. They can also be extended back as though there was a view to a terrace (fig. 5-21).

Establishing a floor grid from which measurements can be taken is as simple as extending lines from intersections back to the proper vanishing point (fig. 5-22).

In learning two-point perspective, it is always helpful to have a reference handy, since directions of lines can sometimes be confusing, even to the experienced.

Centuries ago the design-conscious Japanese developed paper-folding techniques called origami. Folded paper boxes are a delight to make and serve not only as a handy reference but as props for limitless problems.

Figure 5-23 contains the instructions for making a paper box, as written by a beginning student. (The written directions and the diagrams were part of a graded exercise, with the grade depending on the clarity of the writing and the readability of the diagrams. I will leave it to the reader to decide what grade this example deserved.)

If a whole class has made paper boxes, there will be enough to build models from which to draw. A church is a good beginning. Naves and transepts can be discussed. With enough boxes a church with double towers at the west end and double transepts is possible.

Naturally, paper boxes are not beautifully symmetrical cubes, but they have the advantage of being abundant and are perfect for devising complicated arrangements with which to practice perspective theory.

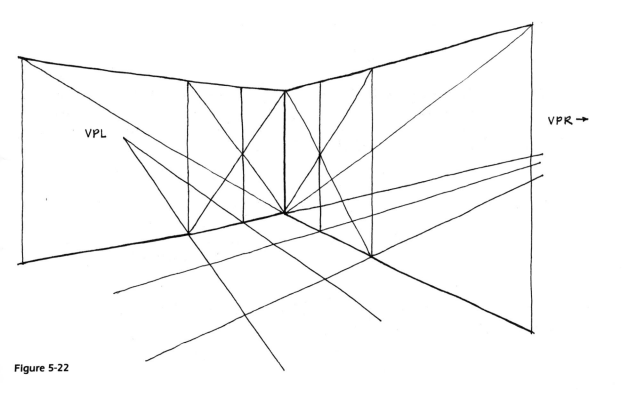

VPL

VPR →

Figure 5-22

**Problem 57:
Drawing of a
box church**

Use a pencil and grid paper. On a table, set up a model church made of paper boxes that is five boxes long, with a transept at box four with a tower on it. Position yourself so that you are seeing the church in two-point perspective. Begin by drawing one box in two-point perspective. Then use the diagonal method to add the rest of the boxes.

You could just as easily make a two-point-perspective grid on which to plot the footprint of the church. Add the tower by using the diagonal method.

Paper boxes are fine props for rendering exercises, in black-and-white or color, in pen or pencil. Care needs to be taken that the subtle light changes on the surface are not exaggerated, or the contrast will be too great (fig. 5-24).

An extension of the origami boxes is a problem I call Box City, made up of a collection of cardboard cartons painted white. In effect it is just an extension of problem 56, but its scale makes it a powerful statement about volume. This set of boxes is head high. It projects a sense of mass, stability, and connection to the ground. It can be assembled as a city with streets and crossings, or it can be an indi-

How to Make a Paper Box

1. Begin with a square sheet of paper. If square paper is not available, a regular sheet of paper may be used. Fold it on the diagonal and remove the paper that is not doubled.

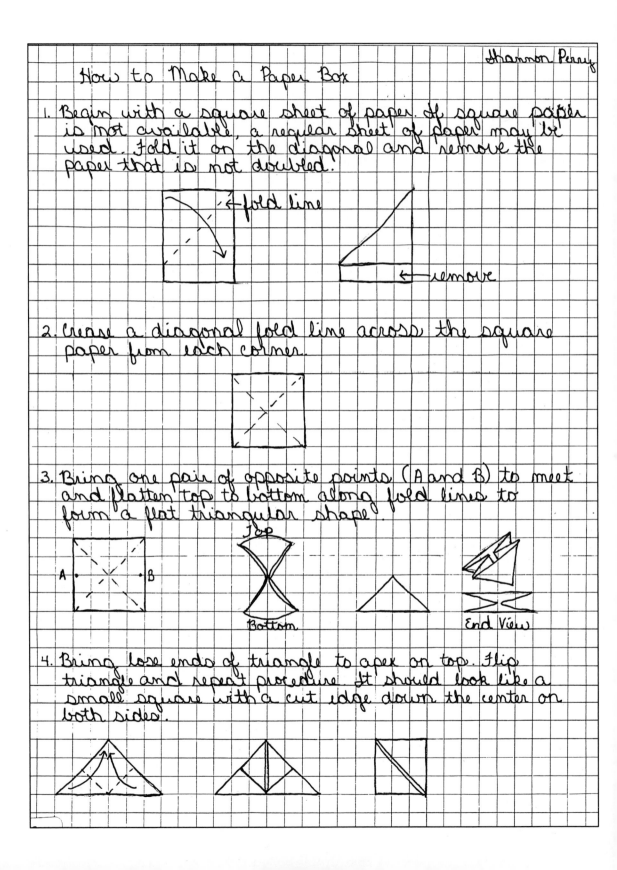

2. Crease a diagonal fold line across the square paper from each corner.

3. Bring one pair of opposite points (A and B) to meet and flatten top to bottom along fold lines to form a flat triangular shape.

4. Bring lose ends of triangle to apex on top. Flip triangle and repeat procedure. It should look like a small square with a cut edge down the center on both sides.

5. Fold the points with two folded edges and a cut edge down the center to that edge. Do the same on the other side. Both sides should be identical.

6. Take loose flaps of the long central part and fold them to where the fold is directly along the edge of the small triangle.

7. Fold the flap that hangs over the paper back up on top of itself, forming a small triangle on top of a larger one. Tuck this smaller triangle inside the larger one. Do this on both sides of the paper.

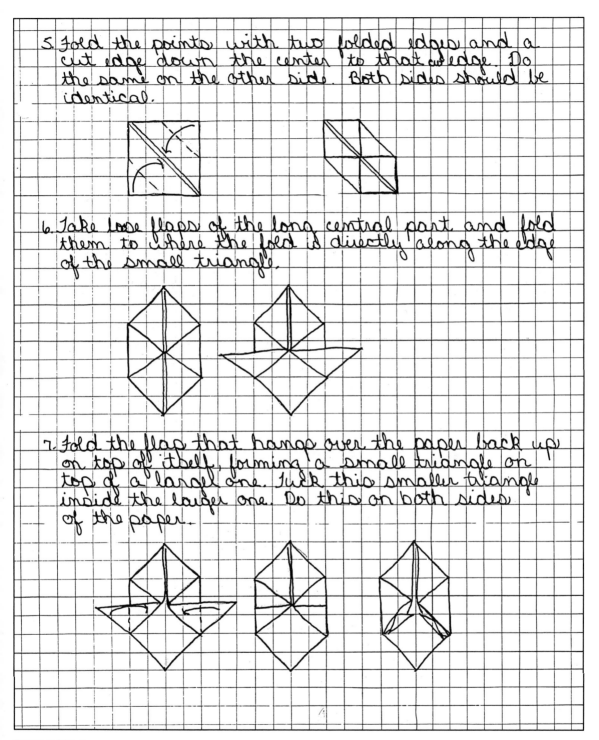

Figure 5-23a, b

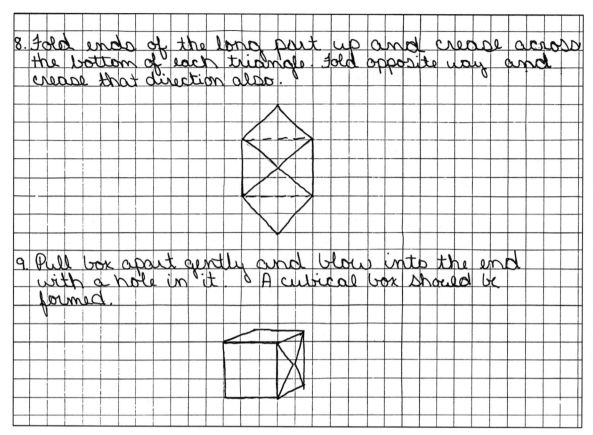

8. Fold ends of the long part up and crease across the bottom of each triangle. Fold opposite way and crease that direction also.

9. Pull box apart gently and blow into the end with a hole in it. A cubical box should be formed.

Figure 5-23c

vidual structure. Students can be asked to draw its footprint, requiring them to move around to view it from all angles. It provides an equally good lesson in sections, both vertical and horizontal. Primarily, however, its value is as a setup for perspective drawing. A sitting person sees the assemblage on the eye level, below the eye level, and above the eye level. A whole class can group around, and there are unlimited views.

Problem 58: Drawing of Box City

Use a pencil and grid paper. Position yourself so that you are looking at the boxes in two-point perspective. You will be attempting to draw this complex as you see it, so the location of your eye level is extremely important. If you begin with a box that is sitting on the floor, chances are that by the time you get to the upper boxes, your eye level will not be in the right place. Therefore it might be wise to start with a box that is on the eye level. Then the rest of the boxes can be calculated above or below, where their position is less critical. (See fig. 5-25.)

Problem 59 is a good one to reinforce some of the principles that have been covered so far.

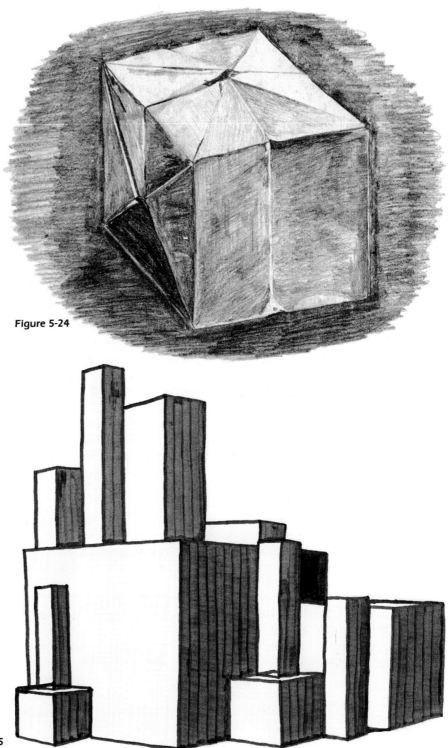

Figure 5-24

Figure 5-25

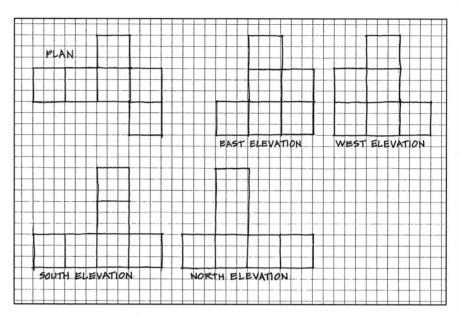

Figure 5-26

Problem 59:
Two-point
perspective from
a plan and four
elevations

Use a pencil and grid paper. Figure 5-26 shows a plan and four elevations: east, west, north, and south. Draw the described structure in two-point perspective, showing all construction lines. Use a high eye level so that all the units will show in your drawing.

Before you can draw you must determine what the structure looks like, based on the elevations. Sometimes trial and error is the only way. Make tiny paraline sketches of the first level of units, and then add the second and third levels. Do not start your page-sized drawing until you are sure of your solution. (See fig. 5-27.)

VANISHING POINTS

It matters not how many stories, sides, bays, cantilevers, overhangs, skylights, or runways a structure or structures have: when the sides of the units are parallel to each other, they will vanish at the same two points. However, the moment a plane is no longer parallel, it will need to have different vanishing points (fig. 5-28).

Problem 60:
Drawing of
boxes at
different angles

Use a pencil and grid paper. On a table arrange four paper boxes so that they are at different angles from each other. You should be looking at all of them in two-point perspective. Draw them. Two different vanishing points will be necessary for each box.

Look at the angle formed by the corner of a box where it meets the table and try to reproduce the angle. Extend the line of the angle to a horizon line. Once you have established a horizon line, all vanishing points will be upon it. Becoming good at seeing angles is part of successful freehand drawing.

Shade may be added to the boxes.

Figure 5-27

Figure 5-28

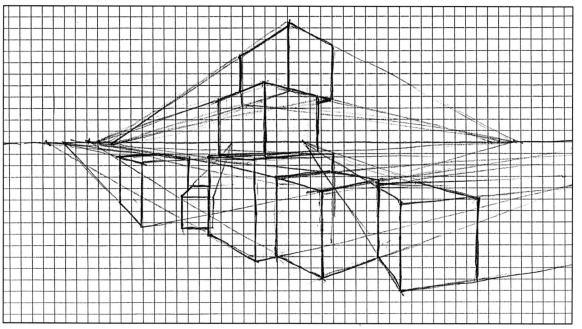

Figure 5-29

Figure 5-30

In freehand drawing laying in a complex building with ranks of windows and files of bays, light lines should be drawn to the vanishing points along all major horizontal divisions. Since at least one of the vanishing points will be well off the page, it sometimes helps to turn the paper so that you yourself are the vanishing point, the center of the universe, and all the lines are coming together at your navel. It is easier to judge the proper convergence of lines if the fan is coming toward you.

Figures 5-29, 5-30, and 5-31 were drawn outdoors by beginning students in a graphic fundamentals class.

The drawing of the outdoor theater in figure 5-32 is one of the last projects of a semester. Obviously it is a problem that cannot be translated to this book. But it has some very special stumbling blocks that are applicable to many drawings of buildings.

One is a misleading length-to-height ratio. This affords an opportunity to introduce students to a mechanical method for better accuracy. By holding a pencil out, stiff-armed, and closing one eye, a vertical measurement can be made against the pencil: the distance between the thumb and the tip of the pencil. Holding on to this measurement and turning the pencil on its side will enable the length of the building to be estimated. The number of heights it takes to make the length is a ratio that can be translated to the drawing page.

Another object lesson in this problem is the eye level. The class was sitting on a knoll approximately on the level of the top of the curving colonnade. Amateurs almost always draw curving colonnades with a bowed top, even when the top of the colonnade is on the eye level. The rule is that any horizontal line will appear horizontal if it is on the eye level, whether it is curving or not.

Last but not least is the perspective of the stepped seating. Circular rows of seating, viewed from directly opposite, will appear as horizontal lines. Only as the rows turn to the right and left do the lines begin to angle down (fig. 5-33).

Figure 5-31

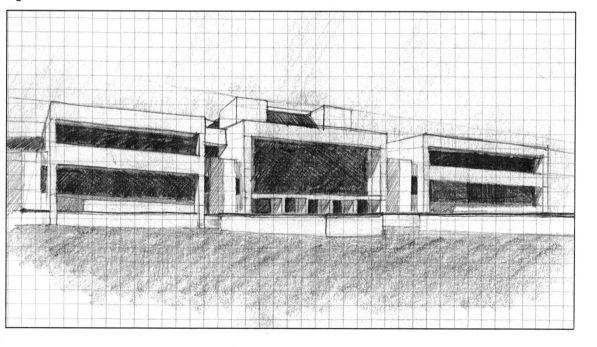

Figure 5-32

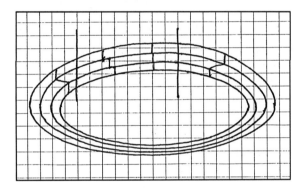

Figure 5-33

When drawing in the studio, good use can be made of whatever building or site models happen to be left over from other projects. It is good practice to draw these on gridded paper to help with the verticals. Other shortcuts can also save time. For example, once the rectangle of the base of the model has been laid out, the relative heights of the various units can be judged against a horizontal pencil (fig. 5-34). Also, looking carefully at how much of the tops of the rectangular shapes can be seen (and drawing them that way) will establish an accurate eye level.

MOVABLE-PLANE PERSPECTIVE

At some point it will be necessary to draw a long building in one-point perspective. As one contemplates how to begin, it becomes clear that only the part of the building that is directly in front of you is in fact in one-point perspective. You must turn your head left and right to see the far ends of the building, and when you do that, you will see both the facade and a side view (fig. 5-35).

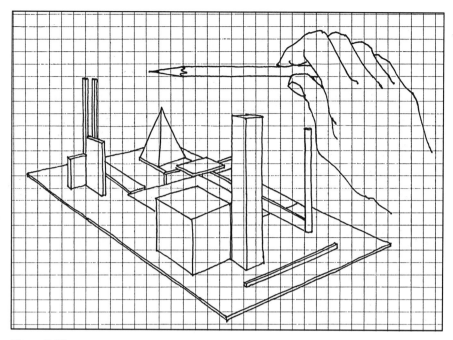

Figure 5-34

By definition, seeing both front and side identifies a two-point perspective, not a one-point perspective. To draw the side wings in two-point perspective and the center in one-point perspective will produce a building that arcs forward in the middle (fig. 5-36).

Such distortion will occur any time the magic circle that represents our cone of vision is exceeded. *Cone of vision* refers to the limited area that we see clearly, directly in front of us. In real life we move our head to shift the cone of vision. On paper we cannot change points of view without either making a separate drawing or showing gross distortion. A fish-eye photograph is an example of the distortion that occurs when the seen view extends far beyond the image from a single viewpoint.

Two different approaches can be used to solve the problem. One is simply to proceed with a one-point perspective, keeping all horizontals horizontal and parallel, but angling the side lines to converge toward the one vanishing point. Or we can minimize some of the distortion by using a movable-plane perspective.

Movable planes are sometimes called *glide projections*. Glides are another way of mechanically constructing an image to convey information. Whereas, in a one-point perspective, the station point (where the viewer is standing) is fixed, in a glide it is on a track running parallel to the picture plane. A glide projection is somewhere between a perspective and a paraline drawing. As with the other projections, when it is used in freehand drawing, it is greatly abbreviated.

A movable-plane drawing has limitations. It is best for showing plans, sections, or facades that are long and shallow. A shallow depth of field is assumed in glide projections.

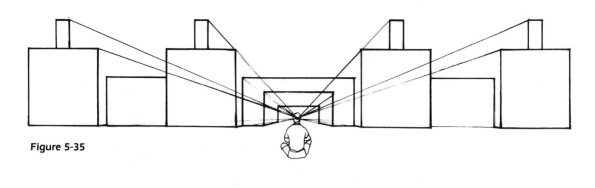

Figure 5-35

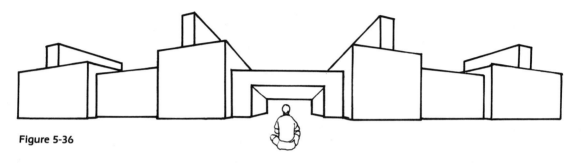

Figure 5-36

**Problem 61:
Movable-plane
drawing of a
skyline**

Use a pencil and grid paper. Draw a skyline in elevation. Add a horizon line and a vanishing point. From the vanishing point, drop a vertical line to some distance below the ground line. Tick the vertical line off in equal increments, beginning at the vanishing point. Every visible side plane of the buildings will have a sight line to the vertical.

Starting at the vanishing point, move right (or left), bringing a line from the top corner of each unit, in order, to successive ticks on the vertical line. Follow the same procedure on the other side of the vanishing point. You will notice that this has the effect of softening the extreme perspective of the one-point system (fig. 5-37).

A depth indicator now must be established. Draw a horizontal line through the first tick mark above the ground line. This can be called a depth line. Lightly drop every major vertical line down to the ground line and then extend it back up to the horizon line, meeting the line coming from the top of the vertical, forming a triangle. The intersection of the line from the ground line with the depth line will mark the position of a vertical that identifies the depth of the building sides (fig. 5-38).

If you think the drawing needs more depth, raise the horizontal depth line to the second tick mark, but bear in mind that movable-plane perspectives are best with a shallow depth of field.

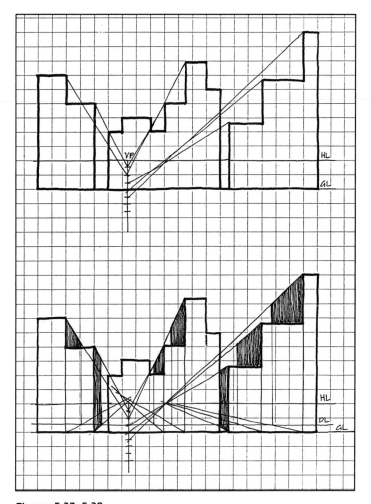

Figures 5-37, 5-38

**Problem 62:
Movable-plane
drawing for a
plan or site plan**

Use a pencil and grid paper. A slightly different system is used for a glide view of a plan. Enclose the view in a rectangle that will include the major outside lines (fig. 5-39). Put in a horizon line and a vertical vanishing line at the station point. Connect the top and bottom corners of the rectangle to points on the vanishing line with lines crossing the horizon line.

All corners on the top line of the rectangle will vanish at the low point on the vanishing line, and all corners on the bottom line of the rectangle will vanish at the high point on the vanishing line. Each set of two lines that will form the sides of the structures will vanish at the point of intersection on the horizon line made by the lines from the top and bottom corners. Hence, all sides horizontal to the viewer will vanish along the vertical (fig. 5-40).

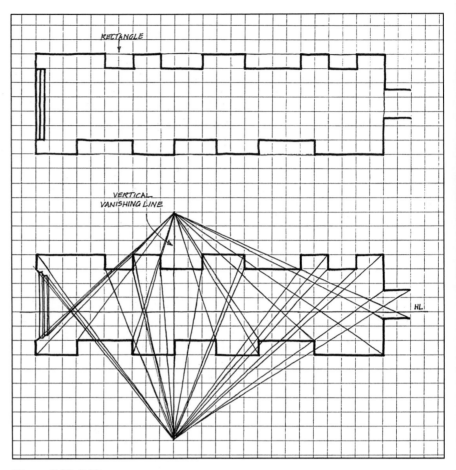

Figures 5-39, 5-40

Figure 5-41

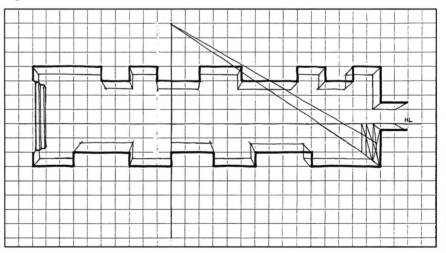

Estimate the first line for depth, remembering that in movable planes, shallowness is preferable. If additional depth is desired, the diagonal line method can be used (fig. 5-41).

SIMPLIFIED MOVABLE-PLANE PROJECTION FOR STAGE SETS

The world does seem to beat a path to architects' doors. They are frequently asked to design furniture, lighting fixtures, children's toys, stained glass, and other consumer goods, and they always take on the task as though born to it. If a town has a community theater, it is an architect who is most often called upon to design the stage sets. It is an exciting and fun project, which should never be turned down.

Designing for the theater requires imagination and that suspension of disbelief that characterizes the world of entertainment. The stage set is a realm of make-believe in which departures from reality, patently impossible angles, and structural inconsistencies can exist without undue audience anxiety. Nonetheless, a perspective framework should underlie the design.

All sets on a proscenium stage must fit within the rectangle of the stage area. Another given is that the sides of the set must be raked (turned in) so that the sight lines from the far right and far left seats will not be totally impeded.

Problem 63:
Simplified
movable-plane
projection for
stage sets

Use a pencil and grid paper. Assign a value of 1 foot to the grid squares. Draw a plan of a stage that is a rectangle 30 by 14 feet (fig. 5-42). A 3-foot rake on either side of the back wall (points A) will make the back wall 24 feet wide, allowing adequate sight lines from the side seats.

The proscenium arch, or the actual opening of the front of the stage, will reveal an interior space that itself may be either an interior or an exterior view. Let us consider an interior setting first.

Draw the proscenium arch underneath the plan on your page by extending the outside lines down. Make the space 14 feet high. Tick off units representing the feet on the left side.

Normally any composition drawn within this rectangle would be in one-point perspective; however, this will produce a view in which the angles are unhappily steep and the perceived depth greatly exaggerated. This distortion makes the stage set a perfect place to use a simplified version of movable planes.

Begin by placing two vanishing points on a vertical line centered within the rectangular frame. The points should divide the line into thirds. Connect the top vanishing point to the right and left top corners of the rectangular frame (the proscenium arch), and the bottom vanishing point to the bottom right and left corners of the frame. Now, referring to the floor plan, "cheat" the back corners of the set 3 feet toward the center on either side (points B). This is to give the walls some perspective in addition to the raking that allows for good sight lines. Drop lines from points B to the set, forming the back corners of the wall. Horizontals will complete the back wall.

Tick off a measure between the two vanishing points, and connect the lines with the equivalent vertical measure on the proscenium arch. All points on the side walls will vanish along the vanishing line between the two points. Back-wall measure-

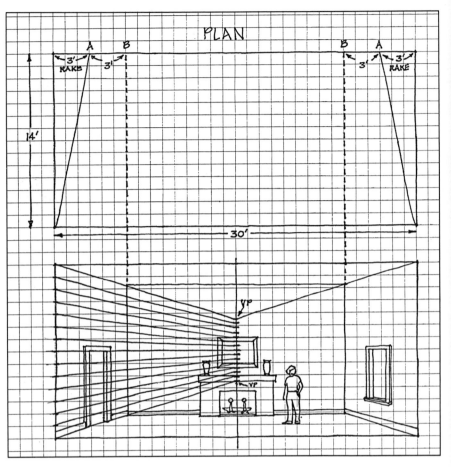

Figure 5-42

ments are taken from measuring lines as they cross the back corners. Add a scale figure.

A similar procedure works for an exterior setting. Remember that scale must correspond to the height of the actors, to be determined by the vertical scale on the proscenium arch. If it is desirable to show a distant view of a house or trees, it would be wise to separate them from the acting area by a wall or a hedge so that one does not see a person standing next to a house or tree that is only three or four feet tall.

Make a final drawing using the above dimensions at a $1/2$-inch scale. This will give you a plan that is 15 by 7 inches and a proscenium that is also 15 by 7 inches, a nice drawing size.

A drawing like the final drawing in problem 63 is all that is needed for a presentation to a director or a little theater board. It is also sufficient for the set builder, who knows what must be done next.

6.

Drawing from Reproductions, Slides, Still Lifes, and Nature

So far most of the drawing exercises in this book have entailed learning how to draw with formulas. The formulas, which are essential for professionals, call for a certain capability with pen or pencil, but they do little to inspire creativity.

Certainly drawing is a means for making ideas visible, but it should also be an instrument of creativity itself—a means of producing ideas where none were before.

This kind of drawing does not happen by accident. It requires the disciplining of eye and hand before the eye and the hand will respond automatically to an inner call. Such training can take many forms, but one that is convenient for a studio class is to draw from reproductions or slides of great works of art, practicing drawing techniques and at the same time learning the whys and wherefores of outstanding design.

We study masterpieces of art and architecture to learn why they are great, to become familiar with the qualities that give inspiration to an image, beginning with an analysis of form. We train the eye to see the balance of parts and the hand to interpret them accurately.

DRAWING FROM REPRODUCTIONS

Cartesian coordinates enable us to locate any spot on a two-dimensional grid by a simple method that can be thought of as "over" and "up." The X axis tells how many units "over" a point is; the Y axis tells how many units "up" it is. In figure 6-1, point A is located at the intersection of 2X and 3Y; point B is at the intersection of 3X and 2Y. The grid may be subdivided as often as necessary to locate any point.

To make a sketch of a photograph or a drawing is as simple as visualizing a mental grid on top of the image and estimating where certain crucial points fall. Many drawings and painting are already ordered with verticals and horizontals that only need to be carefully observed as to placement. This theory is simple enough, but it does require serious thought on the part of the artist or designer.

In making a drawing from a photograph or another drawing, the outside border should be drawn first. It is important that it be carefully represented because the rest of the drawing will hinge on its accuracy. Many questions must be answered. Is it a

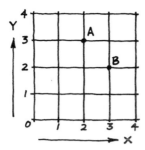

Figure 6-1

square, a rectangle? Is it twice as long as it is high? How does the image fit into the frame?

Mentally dividing the image in half both vertically and horizontally will establish where important points or lines are. The image should be viewed as though it were simply a collection of edges, lines, points, and intersections.

Problem 64: Drawing of the painting *The Messenger of Autumn,* by Paul Klee

The original painting is at the Yale University Art Gallery, New Haven, Connecticut. The composition, drawn in figure 6-2, is both architectonic and musical in its organization. Its serene planes suggest the days fading into autumn, embracing the tree symbol and echoing the lunar arc.

What is the shape of the overall image? A fat horizontal rectangle. Does the design relate to a simple halving of the space, vertically and horizontally? Yes, but . . . . As soon as we consider the vertical, we notice something amiss. The lines are neither truly vertical nor horizontal. Klee was not interested in ruler-true lines, knowing that a line drawn against a straightedge lacks soul. A machine can draw a straight line. We must be more than machines.

Use a pencil and grid paper. Draw the border. Within the border draw the vertical divisions, and add one or two major horizontals. Draw the block with the tree and the block with the arc next. Relate them to each other by checking their relative position on the page. Now almost all that remains is to lay in the dozens of horizontal lines, noting those that continue through several columns and those that do not. With the addition of the nine obliques, the composition analysis is complete. (See fig. 6-3.)

Any composition that comprises predominantly straight lines can be drawn quickly because the lines are easy to locate. What about curving lines, or compositions that do not seem to have any straight lines at all?

Problem 65: Drawing of the painting *Starry Night,* by Vincent van Gogh

The famous painting *Starry Night,* by Vincent van Gogh, is in the collection of The Museum of Modern Art in New York City. As shown in the drawing of it in figure 6-4, there is hardly a straight line in it, yet it seems to fall naturally into a division of two horizontals and two verticals, on either side of the bisections.

Use a pencil and grid paper. Draw the shape of the rectangular border. Lightly bisect it horizontally and vertically. Visualize this simple grid on top of the painting.

Figure 6-2

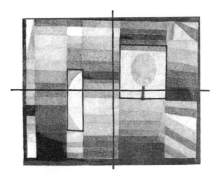

Figure 6-3

Figure 6-4

Figure 6-5

The major line of the distant hills slopes up from below the halfway line to close to the halfway line on the right. The major line of the sworls in the sky is almost parallel to the line of the hills. The cypress trees form the major vertical line, echoed by a less clear division through the sworls and down past the church tower. (See fig. 6-5.)

This accurate outline will allow you to relax and put all your effort into treatment of the surface. If the framework is accurate enough, even a poor rendering will not prevent instant recognition of the image.

DRAWING FROM SLIDES

Drawing from slides is essentially no different than drawing from reproductions. It is an excellent means of practice, and many opportunities present themselves, particularly in a classroom situation. Slides of any kind of building can be used, since the drawing principles remain the same.

All art or architecture history classes should be attended with notebook in hand, the better to capture the elusive slide. Gridded paper helps, although a small notebook is a better tool in a classroom. Pen is more practical than pencil, as it does not smear and shows up better in the dark.

Figures 6-6 and 6-7 show two pages of super-quick sketches from slides, each done by a beginning student.

Problem 66:
Quick sketches
from slides

Use a pen and grid paper. The drawings will be made from slides showing masterpieces of Western architecture. Each slide will be exhibited for less than one minute.

Since speed is of the essence in such a situation, you must strive to capture the essentials. Do not begin a sketch with stair rails or window mullions. *Identification* is the operative word. Identification depends absolutely on accurate proportion and scale, not on details, even if there were time to add them.

Identification sketches must always be kept very small, not only because of the speed requirement, but because, as drawings get larger, it is necessary to add more detail, and more detail detracts from, rather than encourages, recognizability.

It is not easy to transform a photograph or a slide into a diagram. One tends to put in the details first because they seem to be the easiest. Everyone can draw window mullions, whereas determining the basic shape that is hiding behind a lot of ornament is daunting.

In identification sketches one must put aside perspective, forget details, and concentrate on the geometric shape of the structure. Even a slide as complicated as one showing Saint Peter's Basilica can be diagramed if the basic shape is seen as a long rectangle with a small pediment identifying the honorific entrance. A long, low rectangle with square windows forms the second story. The sculpture and the small domes on the roof can be ignored, as they are not important; but the shape of Michelangelo's dome, rising from a tall drum and topped with a substantial cupola, is critical. The sketch of the basilica shown in figure 6-8 took twenty seconds to complete.

What about another complicated image, such as the facade of the Notre-Dame of Paris? It is no more than a collection of horizontal stripes. The first one, on the bottom, contains the three portals; the narrow one above is the sculptured row of all the kings of France; then comes the medium one with the rose window; next, a narrow one of colonnades; and finally the two squared-off towers with the steeple in between. The sketch shown in figure 6-9 took fifteen seconds to complete.

Even the very complex slide, such as one of the Hagia Sophia, can be drawn in less than half a minute. First, the shape of the dome—flattened—on top of a low drum, set on the square bulk of the building, is drawn. Then comes the two massive original buttresses flanking the blind arch. A half dome on either side, four mina-

Figure 6-6

Figure 6-7

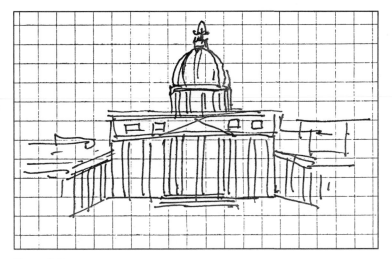

Figure 6-8

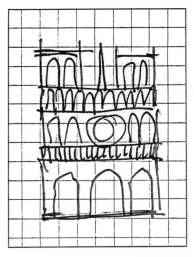

Figure 6-9

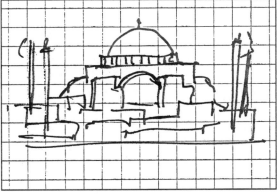

Figure 6-10

rets, and higgledy-piggledy lines for the outbuildings complete the sketch. The sketch shown in figure 6-10 required twenty-five seconds to complete.

Diagrammatic sketches aside, drawing from slides is the same as drawing from a painting, except for scale. Once it is clear to a student that drawing is simply copying what you see in front of you, all sorts of obstacles vanish. The plaintive complaint, "I can't draw people (cars, trees, buildings)," will be heard less often.

Art teachers have known for years that the mind gets in the way of drawing. If, for example, I were to tell students to draw a simple portrait of their neighbor, I would be met with hysteria. Thoughts of public humiliation, inadequacy, and scorn would remove any hope of a reasonable drawing. Even as simple a shape as a chair carries mental baggage that makes accurate rendition difficult.

Ideas on how to cope with this fear have been stockpiled through the years. One of the best is to try to disguise the image. Turn the slide upside down and have students draw the inverted picture. They will shortly discover that their drawings are more accurate when they rely only on direction and slant of lines rather than drawing a house the way they think they know a house should be. Figures 6-11 and 6-12 show two drawings of the same slide. The slide used for figure 6-11 was upside down; that for 6-12, right side up. Figure 6-11 is clearly in better proportion than figure 6-12 is. Figure 6-13 is another page of student drawings with only one drawn right side up.

This exercise can be broken down even further, to good effect. Using an inverted slide, lead the students through construction, line by line, insisting that each line be placed just so before continuing. The end result is 100 percent success and a meaningful object lesson. Figures 6-14, 6-15, and 6-16 are other examples of very quick student drawings (less than two minutes) made from upside-down slides.

Figure 6-11

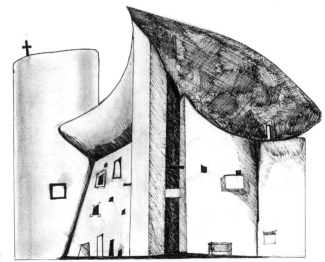

Figure 6-12

Figure 6-13

Figure 6-14

Figure 6-16

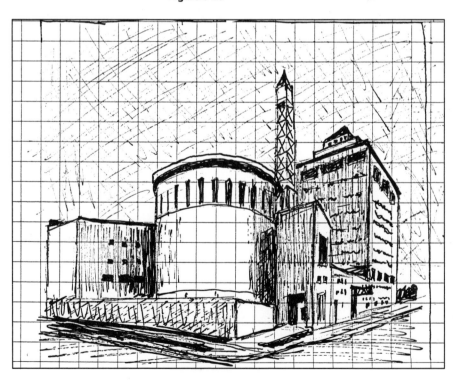

Figure 6-15

Another excellent exercise is to project the slide just enough out of focus to eliminate the small details, forcing attention on the big picture and cutting down on the common tendency to start by drawing window mullions. Squinting at the projection will achieve the same result but is harder to sustain.

In preparing for a future in architecture or an allied profession, accuracy and speed in drawing are more important than style is. Style will follow in due course. Knowing that a sketch will be recognizable instead of wildly distorted, that the viewer will say, "That's good," instead of, "What is it?" fosters confidence that begets more skill.

PATTERNS OF LIGHT AND SHADE IN QUICK SKETCHES

Sometimes a view will be so complex that the thought of drawing it causes despair in the hearts of students. Instead of focusing the mind on an underlying structure, panic ensues.

Four exercises can be used to treat this syndrome. All are wickedly complicated. The message is that, if it is possible to deal with these, then anything is possible.

The first is a slide of Moshe Safdie's housing project Habitat from the 1967 World's Fair in Montreal, Canada. Well sunlit, it is a mountain of dark and light squares, long and short diagonals, all liberally sprinkled with black checks. Pen will be the tool; otherwise, there will be nothing but furious erasing for fifteen minutes.

Problem 67:
Quick drawing
of Habitat

Use pen and grid paper. The slide of Habitat will be shown for only fifteen minutes.

There is no way to represent this structure literally in only fifteen minutes. The only hope is to concentrate first on a quick outline of the "mountain," and then to fill in the large pattern of shadow, seeing it as a blob of a certain shape that moves up and to the right, becoming attenuated to the left. Do not attempt to draw the units of the structure; there is no time. Squinting the eyes will help the shape of the major shadow to stand out from the other complications. Estimate the slant of the diagonals and slash them in. Remember that the slant represents the angle of the sun, and so it will be the same slant on all of the front surfaces. A few squares can be added around the edge. If time allows, some window dots can be added. Voila! (See fig. 6-17.)

The second exercise is a related one. Using a pile of paper boxes, make a mound loosely similar to Habitat, and train a floodlight on it. That this is real life, not a slide, adds another dimension of difficulty to the problem.

Problem 68:
Quick drawing
of a pile of boxes

Use pen and grid paper. Do a lot of squinting for this one, as it is one of the few ways to reduce the complexity of an image to its major components—in this case, its light and shade. There is absolutely no way to draw this composition, box by box, fifteen minutes, so a different strategy has to be used. Even starting with the outline will not work well because there is not a clear pattern of shadow, as there was in problem 67. Begin instead with many vertical lines and dark polygons. First draw the big boxes quickly, and then fill in small polygons as fast as possible. Do not count or attempt any particular placement of the boxes. You are striving for effect. (See fig. 6-18.)

The third problem is a slide of the town of Casares, in Spain. It is a waterfall of tile roofs cascading down a hillside, infinitely intricate.

Again, there is no way to reproduce the reality of the image in fifteen minutes. The shape of the shadows looks like saw-toothed ribbons repeated in lockstep. If the repeating pattern can be stroked out quickly and rhythmically, success will be at hand.

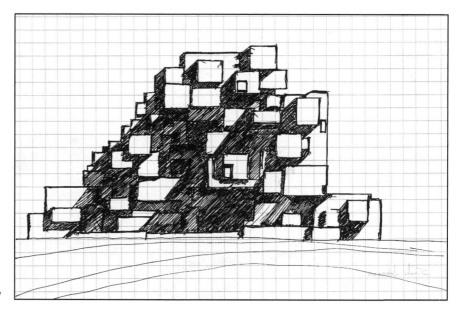

Figure 6-17

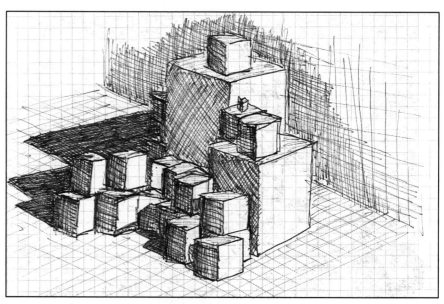

Figure 6-18

Use a pen and grid paper. Notice that the pattern of shadow looks like descending stairsteps. Fill in a stairstepped ribbon with black. Add another stairstepped ribbon and fill it with alternating gray and white shapes. Only by establishing this pattern and following it quickly without regard to the individual units as seen in the slide can the drawing be completed. (See fig. 6-19.)

The last problem involves drawing from a chipboard model. The model has approximately the same conformation as the preceding images, with many planes of varying heights, juxtaposition of walls and roofs, terraces and stairs. This time, no

Figure 6-19

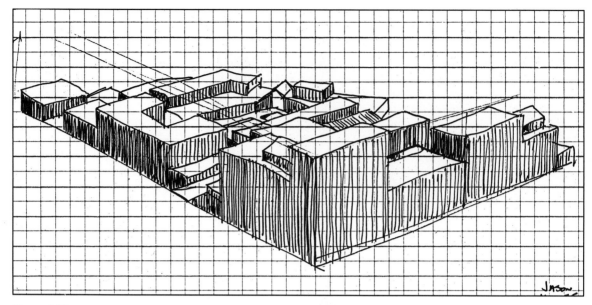

Figure 6-20

strong light is available to help with the skeleton. A different pattern needs to be seen. Most students decide on a modified grid approach that is both quick and responsive to the model.

Problem 70: Quick drawing of a chipboard model

Use a pen and grid paper. Put the model on a table. Situate yourself so that you are looking at the model in two-point perspective. Since this is real life and the model is being viewed from above, the first step is to judge the angle of the near corner. All the horizontal lines going to the left will be almost parallel to the left side of the angle, and all the horizontal lines going to the right will be almost parallel to the right side of the angle.

Look to see if there are any natural divisions in the composition, and let them establish a kind of grid. Stairstep many varying heights quickly on either side, and shade at least one set of sides. Do not attempt to draw the model as it really is—there will not be time. You want to give the impression of a multilevel three-dimensional construction. (See fig. 6-20.)

DRAWING FROM STILL LIFES

Faced with an arrangement of objects to draw, the most immediate need is to decide how much of the composition to draw. A quick frame made with the fingers will create a tiny view from which to make a judgment (fig. 6-21). Moving the fingers closer to the eye increases the scope of the subject matter. Even better is an empty slide frame (fig. 6-22).

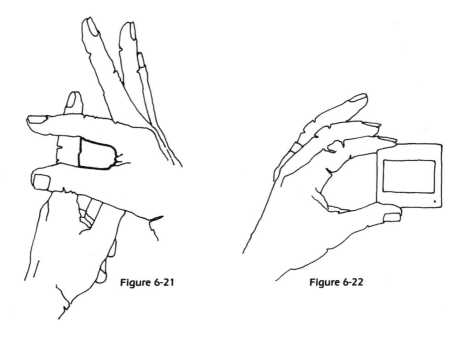

Figure 6-21

Figure 6-22

Problem 71:
Still-life drawing

Use a pencil and grid paper. Set up a still life that includes a chair or table or some-thing with legs, along with several other objects.

To begin, find an important point in the still-life arrangement that is in the center or somewhere along a vertical or horizontal line bisecting the arrangement. Relate the composition to the bisectors. See everything as a collection of lines and points, to relate them better.

The bottoms of objects can be a source of anxiety. "How do I make that leg look like it is behind that base?" Look only at the lines or points of the bottoms as you see them; as they would, in fact, appear on a grid. Is point A higher up on the page than point B? How far above? How much higher up on the page is point C than point D? (See fig. 6-23.)

After these major lines and points have been established, the rest of the drawing is built up by following lines or edges and relating them to those already in place.

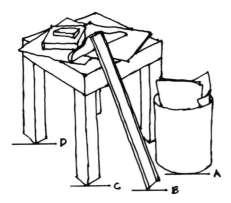

Figure 6-23

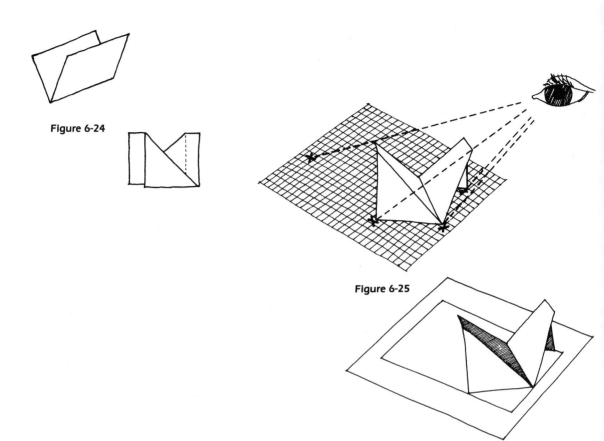

Figure 6-24

Figure 6-25

Practice in relating points and lines is at the heart of drawing the world as we see it. The following problem reinforces that principle while also stressing straight lines and attention to detail.

Problem 72: Construction and drawing of a module

Use a pencil and grid paper. A module is a unit that is repeated identically. Fold a 5- by 8-inch lined index card in half widthwise, with the lines on the inside. Fold one corner down to the fold line. Turn the card over and fold the other corner to the fold line (fig. 6-24). You now have an interesting module to place in front of you on a piece of gridded paper. Place it close to the bottom of the page, arranging it on its points or edges, not on one of its planes. You are going to draw a frame for the module whose dimensions will be established by your careful observation of the module as it sits in front of you.

Decide the size of the frame by visualizing where the module touches it. The frame needs to touch the module at one point, and only one point, on each of the four sides. The bottom is easy because the module really does touch the border there. It may actually touch one of the sides as well, but for at least the topmost point and probably one side, you must close one eye and decide where the point *looks like* it will touch the top of the frame. How far up is it, and how far over? Put a dot on your border at the spot where the module will touch each side. You should now have a rectangle with a dot on each of its four sides (fig. 6-25).

Only now are you to draw the module. Perspective will not be considered in this problem. Some of the dots can be joined directly with a straight line; other points, such as intersections, will have to be calculated in the familiar "how far up and how far over" manner. The accuracy of the completed drawing will depend on the accuracy of your estimates.

The second part of the problem is to draw the printed lines of the index card. The number of lines visible must be counted and the edge to which they are parallel must be located. Establish spacing by dividing the lines in half and in half again until you have the proper number. Draw the lines starting at the edge to which they are parallel. It is easier to keep lines parallel when they can be related to a line that is close by. (See fig. 6-26.)

Figure 6-26

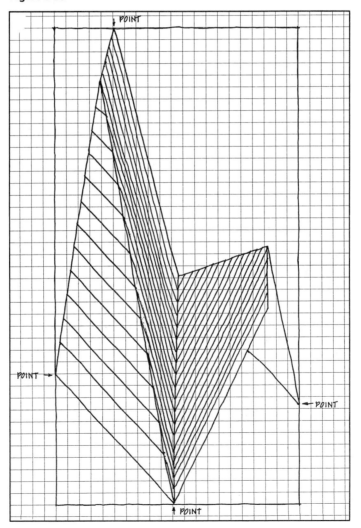

ABOUT VALUE

Most students can hardly wait to start "shading." It is the icing on the cake. Indeed, it is what makes a drawing look real, not to mention attractive; but its most important effect is its ability to give an object *volume*. Only the contrast between light and shade can produce the solid, substantial look of a three-dimensional object. Line drawings never achieve such a look, decorative though they may be.

For architects, landscape architects, and interior designers, it is imperative to understand and be able to execute value handily.

Value indicates how different a color is from pure white or solid black. A *high value* is light, a *low value* is dark. Everything the eye can see has a value. Value is not to be confused with color. Color has value too, and it can be misleading. Think about taking a black-and-white photograph of a colorful scene. In the picture the scene is comprehended easily. In fact, color usually is not even missed, because value provides enough information for the eye/mind to interpret the physical world.

Deciding what is the rule of a bright red sweater, however, presents more of a problem. Fortunately there is a trick that can help. All that is necessary is to squint way down—*way* down—until hardly anything can be seen. This has the effect of limiting the light entering the eye, thus minimizing color and maximizing value. Squinting way down will reveal that red, for example, is low in value. It is very dark. Red, when photographed in black-and-white, prints black. Light blue prints white.

Problem 73:
Value study in pencil

Use a pencil and grid paper. Draw a border around the page, close to the edge. Inside the rectangular border, draw, *very lightly*, two rectangles approximately 2 by 5 inches. Use the grid squares to estimate size.

Shade the background from black to paper white, leaving the two small rectangles blank. Next, shade the two small rectangles in the reverse direction, from paper white to solid black (fig. 6-27). The shading is to be done with the utmost care. It should represent the very best that you are capable of achieving, which means no visible pencil strokes, a gradual and smooth progression from light to dark, and care at the border to keep it clean and sharp.

This may be your first experience with the differences between hard and soft pencils. It is difficult to use a soft pencil for a very light value because, no matter how careful you are, too much carbon is laid down on the paper. Conversely, a hard pencil will not give you a rich, deep black no matter how hard you press; the most it can offer is a silvery gray. The obvious solution is to use a hard pencil in the light areas and a soft one in the dark areas. However, one discovers quickly that there is a color difference between hard and soft pencils that is noticeable on the page. Use pencils that are as close to medium in weight as possible to minimize the color differences. Be patient.

Problem 74:
Value study of a module

The module that was made for problem 72 will be the subject of this exercise. Use a pencil and grid paper. Set up your module, and make your drawing as in problem 71, making sure that your module touches the frame at just one spot on each side.

Figure 6-27

You are practicing your skill at judging the relationship of points and lines. Make your drawing very light.

Look at the module, and squint way down, so that you can easily see the difference in value on the eight planes of the module. One of the planes will be catching the most light. This plane should be left paper color. What is the darkest area? Probably the shadow under the module. What are the planes in between? And what is the value of the background? The background should never be left until last, since its value will have a surprising influence on the rest of the drawing. (See figs. 6-28 and 6-29.)

If this is to be a useful lesson in value, the quality of the pencil rendering is important. After all, if a gray is a scribble with dark and light patches, who knows what the value really is?

ABOUT TECHNIQUE

When the object to be drawn is mechanically smooth and clean with sharp edges, the drawing should probably reflect that characteristic: that is, the object should have a value so smooth that no pencil strokes are visible. Edges need special care. One can always use the edge of an erasing shield to draw against.

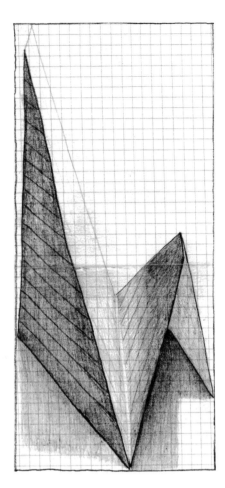

Figure 6-29

Figure 6-28

Very light values are the most difficult to represent. Very soft pencils lay down too much carbon, no matter how feather-light the touch. A 3H or 4H pencil would be a good choice. When time permits, the best technique for smoothness is to draw tiny linked circles, gradually covering the whole area (fig. 6-30).

A quicker way of laying down a good medium-to-dark value that has a little texture is to start with blocks of light parallel strokes only about ¹/₂ inch long—the distance that the fingers can move easily without engaging the hand or the wrist. The lines should be as close together as possible, and the blocks should not overlap. The paper is turned, and the technique is repeated until the desired darkness is achieved (fig. 6-31).

Very dark values are best obtained by crosshatching rather than by attempting to press on the pencil hard enough to produce solid blackness. Trying to create solid blackness with pressure will result in a reflective surface, which will be at variance with the other textures on the page. It will also depress the paper and wrinkle it a little. Crosshatching allows a tiny bit of light to show through the lines, even if so many layers have been put down that the paper appears to be solid black.

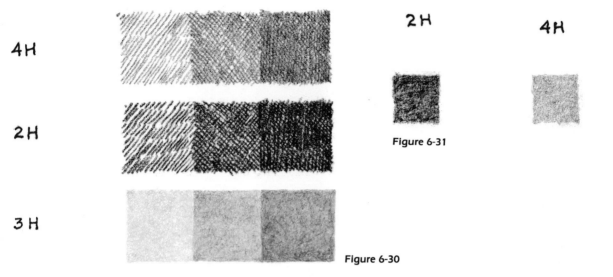

4H

2H

3H

2H

4H

Figure 6-31

Figure 6-30

Problem 75:
Value study of
a paper box

Use a pencil and grid paper. Set a paper box on the table in front of you. The box is more interesting to draw if it is somewhat shopworn. View it in two-point perspective. Lay out the box lightly, making sure it is big enough to fill your page nicely. Draw only as many lines as are needed to position the box and indicate the major folds. Do not waste time making a line drawing when a value study is what is wanted. A value study will require all the time you have.

Decide which is the lightest and which the darkest area of your composition. Make a special point of deciding which value the background is, perhaps even putting it in right away. Squint your eyes to see the values of the sides of the box. Almost surely the top will be the lightest. Cover the whole side with a base value before beginning to fuss with the fold lines; this will keep you from having too much contrast. The temptation is to draw in the wrinkles and the folds with harsh black lines. They must maintain their proper relationship to the other values. (See fig. 6-32.)

RENDERING CURVED SURFACES

The solid shapes out of which most structures can be formed are the sphere, the cube, the cylinder, and the pyramid. The planar forms—the cube and the top of the cylinder—are shaded according to the amount of light they receive, usually in three values: light, medium, and dark.

Curving surfaces contain all three of the values on one surface. The value pattern of light on a sphere and on a cylinder must be memorized.

In rendering a sphere, the light source needs to be located—upper right or upper left—and a disk of paper color (white) left at that spot. Sometimes called the highlight, this represents the lightest area on the sphere. Next is an oval of light shade, and finally the darkest shade, just inside the outer edge of the sphere. At the very edge is a fringe of reflected light (fig. 6-33). Some value added to the background of the drawing will emphasize the reflected light (fig. 6-34).

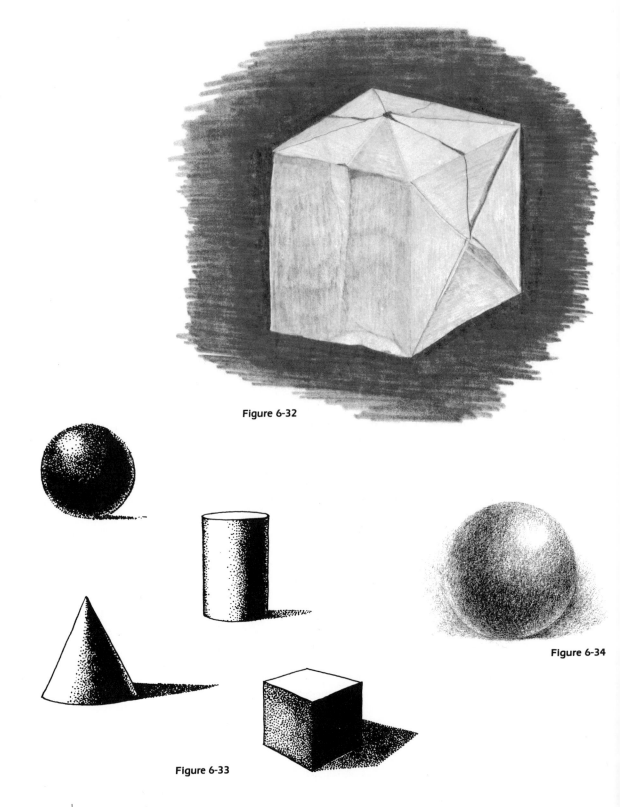

Figure 6-32

Figure 6-34

Figure 6-33

Paper is a wonderful vehicle for catching light on curving surfaces. It combines the softness of the curves with the crisp clarity of cut edges. A long ribbon of cover-stock-weight paper can be stapled to a board for a delightful composition that can be dealt with in part or in full. Drawings can be made first in line, emphasizing the continuous flow of the edges and the uniform width of the ribbon. Then they can be repeated with values. It is a good idea to do these drawings in ink as well as in pencil, because ink forces greater care in observation.

Problem 76:
Line drawing of
a paper curl

The paper curl that has been stapled to the board is a wondrous twisting, turning, undulating work of art. Your composition will show only a part of the whole. Make a frame with your fingers to decide what section of the overall design you like best. It is as important to take in enough as it is not to take in too much. Part of one big curl, for example, would be as dull as dust on the page.

Use a pencil. Grid paper is not necessary. This will be a line drawing, with no shading at all. Allow twenty-five minutes to draw. As you follow the edges of the curl, see where the intersections of lines relate to other important points, using the familiar "how far up and how far over" technique. Putting some pressure on the pencil as it goes around a corner or goes behind something will add life and spirit to the drawing. (See fig. 6-35.)

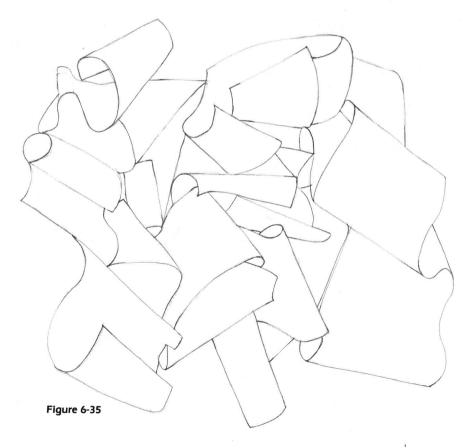

Figure 6-35

**Problem 77:
Value drawing
of a paper curl**

Use a pencil. Choose a different part of the curl to draw, and lay the composition out lightly on your page. This drawing, in light and shade, will be a study in relationships. The ultimate consideration: is one surface lighter or darker than the one next to it? Value studies must rely on lightness and darkness for their conception, not on an outline (fig. 6-36). Outlines have the unsettling habit of reducing even the juiciest of rendered curves into something flat. Notice that in figure 6-37 the curving effect is completely offset by the flattening outline. Nonetheless the drawing is effective as two-dimensional design.

Repeat this problem in pen. It will require a great deal more time to complete, underscoring the difficulty of covering an expanse of paper with skinny pen lines (fig. 6-38). The use of parallel lines in figure 6-39 is one way around this difficulty, though a rather stilted drawing results.

Figure 6-36

Figure 6-37

Figure 6-38

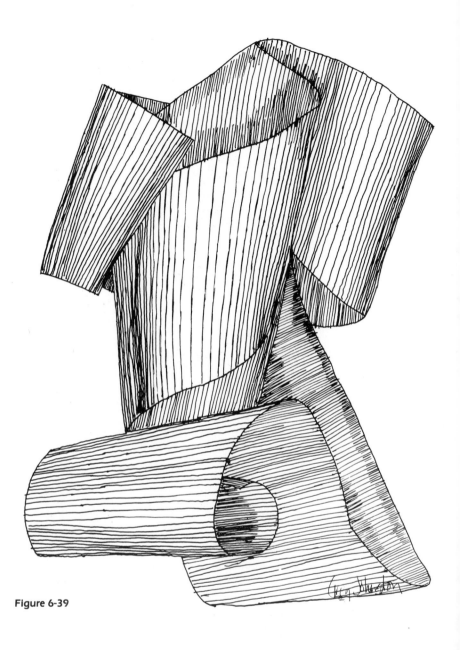

Figure 6-39

Problem 78:
Value drawing
of a paper curl
on contours

Use a pencil. The paper curl has been greatly simplified and pinned on top of a large-scale contour print. The composition need not include the entire setup. Select the area that you find the most interesting, and lay it out lightly on your page. Shadows on the tube shapes will follow the rules for shadows on curved surfaces.

Focus your attention on making the paper curls stand out from the patterned background. Shadows from the curls on the background will help. A difference in the value of the contour lines and the paper curls will also help. (See fig. 6-40.)

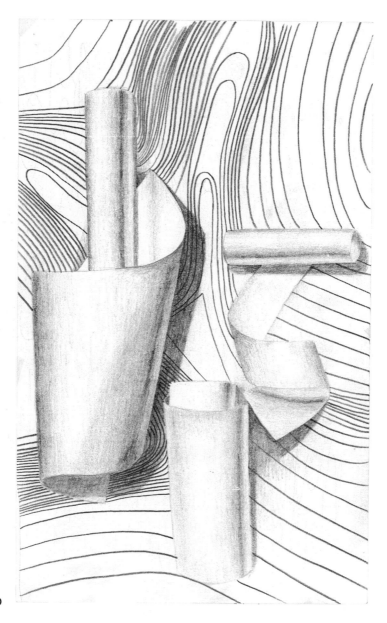

Figure 6-40

Problem 79:
Value study of
an architectural
detail

Use a pen. Grid paper is not necessary. Somewhere on most public buildings are examples of architectural details, perhaps a frieze or column capitals or the bases of lighting fixtures. Position yourself so that your view has light from an angle. Think in terms of three values: light (paper color), medium, and dark. The three values are enough to achieve a feeling of volume. Draw the detail, using only value to define it. (See fig. 6-41.)

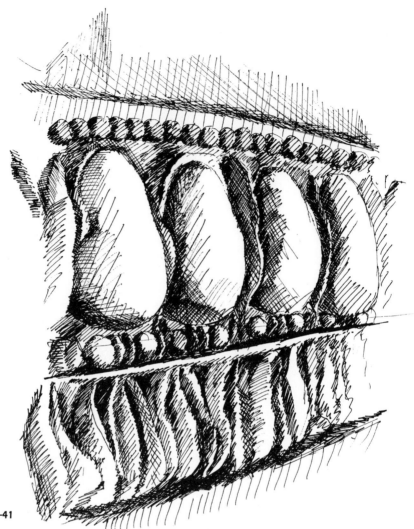

Figure 6-41

Problem 80:
Value study of
a stairwell

Use a pencil and grid paper. Stairwells frequently afford wonderful contrasts in light and shade. This drawing will take at least two hours. It has many more problems to solve than the relatively simple paper curl did. Just laying out the stairs and railing is complicated. Be sure that the perspective is correct, but do not belabor the drawing. It is easy to find yourself developing a line drawing in great detail, forgetting that this is a value study in which you do not want to see outlines. Light planes against darker ones is the formula. Be clear on the relative darkness of a white wall next to the glare of a window. Notice that white window mullions will appear black against the same glare. Is anything darker than the wall just next to the window? Relate all the values. (See figs. 6-42 and 6-43.)

Figure 6-42

Figure 6-43

TEXTURE

Every surface has texture. Most of the surfaces drawn so far in this section have been smooth. Our environment, however, is not made up of smooth surfaces only. Buildings have brick, which is rough, stone, which is lumpy, wood, which is fibrous. The landscape is weedy and layered and granular. Interiors are tweedy and soft and spongy and slick.

It is impossible to practice drawing this wealth of texture, nor is it necessary. What is important is to become sensitive to the qualities of a surface and to develop pencil or pen technique to describe those qualities adequately. Many simple props can be used in a studio to practice the all-important canons of line, point, volume, light and shade, and now texture, including paper bags, fabrics, bottles, and bricks. In contrast to the paper curls drawn previously, which are smooth and rolling and whose edges move without hesitation, rumpled paper bags have a pronounced surface texture.

A cautionary note: in concentrating on texture, one must never forget the underlying structure that supports that surface.

Problem 81:
Value drawing
of a paper bag
in ink

Use a pen. Grid paper is not necessary. The paper bag is a versatile prop. Arrange it to suit yourself, but make sure it is interesting. Folding a cuff down at the top creates a strong set of planes as well as focusing some attention on the mouth, with its hint of interior space.

Move your hand quickly while drawing because many lines are needed to cover the ground. Which is the darkest and which the lightest area? You can be thinking about overall value while your hand is busy building it up. (See fig. 6-44.)

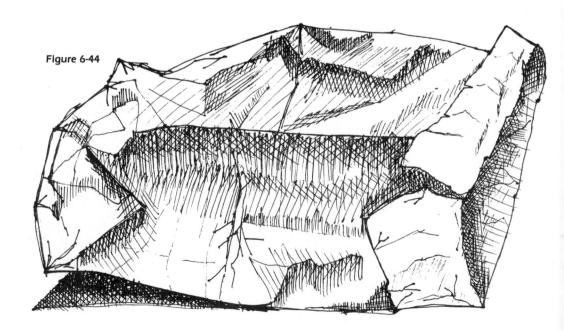

Figure 6-44

Problem 82:
Value study of
many bags

Use a pencil. Grid paper is not necessary. This exercise calls for a lot of paper bags to be stapled to the board; the setup is illuminated from the side by a floodlight.

Concentrate on discerning and depicting a pattern in the values—where are the lightest planes, the darkest? Which of them are similar? A pattern will help to make the drawing intelligible. Do not get bogged down in the small folds and creases before the major planes are clearly delineated. Keep the quality of the paper in mind. Folds, creases, and crumples tend to be straight-lined.

Problem 83:
Fabric study
in ink

Use a pen. Grid paper is not necessary. Arrange a jacket or a sweater on the table in front of you. The entire object need not be drawn, but enough must be on the page to make an interesting composition. Notice the differences between fabric and paper. The values of the fabric are more subtle and the contrasts less sharp than those for paper. The fabric's surface is soft and thick, so that the edges of shadows are not clear. Sweaters or jackets are unlikely to have highlights of a startling white. Modify the highlights accordingly. (See fig. 6-45.)

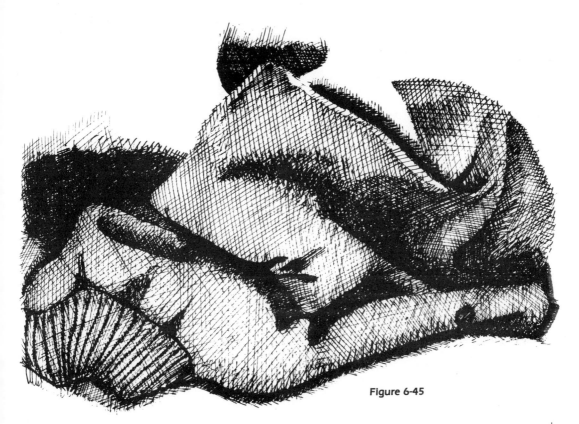

Figure 6-45

Figure 6-46

**Problem 84:
Still life with
texture**

Use a pencil and grid paper. A still-life setup has been provided that will include
fabric as well as some smooth-sided props. Lay in the large shape of the fabric first,
and then use the "how far up and how far over" system to locate the bottle and cans
in their proper proportion. No matter how carefully the texture is rendered, the
drawing will look wrong if its subjects are out of scale.

Your task is to consider surfaces, but the relationship of light and shade is equally
important. What is darkest and what is lightest? Do not forget to put in a background
value to which everything else will relate.

Can you show a difference between the surface of the fabric and the surface of the
can? The shadows on the can should be crisper and harsher than those on the fabric.
The range of light to dark on the fabric will be much less than that on the bottle or
cans. (See fig. 6-46.)

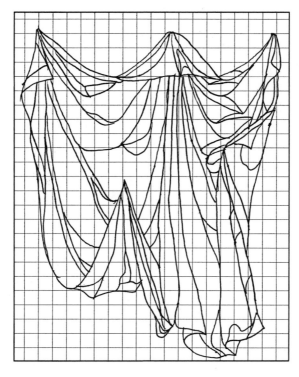

Figure 6-47

Problem 85:
Line drawing
of draped fabric

Use a pen and grid paper. A sheet will be pinned to the board to make an interesting draping pattern.

Use the grid paper to locate where the major points of the composition are in terms of "up and over." Study the way the folds fall from each point of suspension. Your careful drawing of the contours will serve as the framework for a value study. (See figs. 6-47 and 6-48.)

Problem 86:
Value study of
draped fabric

Use pencil and tracing paper. Put tracing paper over your drawing from problem 85 and develop a value study in pencil, using the line drawing as a base.

DRAWING FROM NATURE

Designers draw from nature in order to record places, things, the fleeting moment. They draw from nature to find inspiration—almost all ornament has its roots in natural forms. And they draw outside because nature is the great teacher. A drawing of a tree is wiser if its subject has been studied in reality rather than copied from a book.

Drawing particular objects outside poses few problems, but drawing a landscape does. Most landscapes are drawn by designers for specific reasons, usually for records. The more skillful the recording, the more useful it becomes.

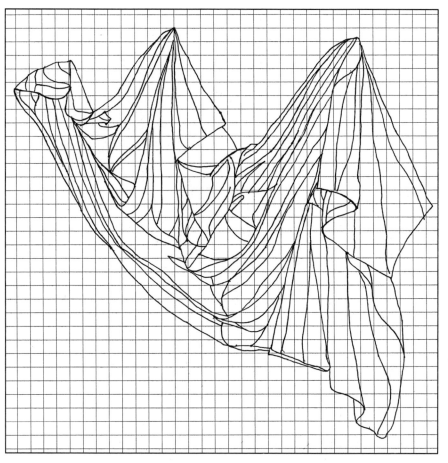

Figure 6-48

BREAKING SPACE INTO MANAGEABLE PARTS

Seeing the infinitely complicated outdoor world in a simple enough fashion to be able to draw it is a challenge. A formula can make it easier and increase speed as well. Break the view into a grid consisting of three divisions of depth: near, middle, and far. Each of the divisions will be treated in a different way. Near subjects will be drawn dark and detailed; those in the middle distance will be lighter and simplified; and those far away will be light and abstract. This formula follows the eye's own interpretation of distance.

The major components of the near division need to be analyzed. Obviously the foreground will be framing the rest of the view, or there would not be any view at all. Objects in the foreground will generally extend outside the field of vision. Trees and buildings extend high up or far to the side. They should be drawn clearly, with detail, and dark.

In the middle ground is where most attention will be focused. If there is a building, the angle of the roof against the sky must be estimated. The ground line in the middle distance is one of the important horizontals. Perhaps there is a tree line in the middle distance that is equally crucial.

The far ground is always the easiest to analyze because all detail is gone. It looks the same as something closer does when squinting at it. Distance is effectively rendered in lighter tones, sometimes with a technique as simple as parallel vertical lines.

The landscape should be viewed as though it were a two-dimensional surface, with the direction of the horizontals and verticals related to a mental grid. "How far up and how far over" is just as true for landscapes as for interior subjects.

Using the near-, middle-, far-ground formula will allow a view to be seen in the same fashion as a slide, except that the boundaries of the composition are not already set (fig. 6-49).

**Problem 87:
Landscape
sketches**
Use a pencil or ink and a gridded pad or notebook. Practice making small diagrammatic sketches of scenes everywhere. These sketches are records, which can be developed at any time into something more detailed. You are practicing the art of simplification, transforming something very complicated into something with all the essentials but none of the detail. Using pen provides better practice than pencil because, with pencil, too much time is spent in erasing.

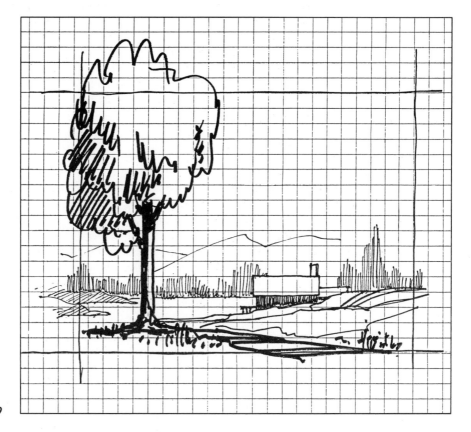

Figure 6-49

REFLECTIONS IN WINDOWS

Windows are an inescapable fact of architectural and interior design life. The actual drawing of the window, either from the outside or the inside, is not difficult. There is a frame and there may be a window covering. The difficulty lies in deciding how to represent the reflections in the glass, particularly from the outside.

Elevation drawings, because they are diagrammatic and not "real" to start with, can be handled by either leaving the window white or filling it in black. Black is perhaps better because it implies something going on behind the window plane.

Perspectives generally demand some treatment that will make the window look as though it has glass in it. What we see in the window glass is composed of the surface of the glass itself, a reflection on that surface, and a view of something behind the surface. Dealing with all of this is a prescription for failure. If, alternatively, the window can be seen as simply a collection of values, success will be at hand. This method is easier said than done, however, because the mind keeps saying, "That lightness is a curtain back there," or "That darkness is the reflection of the tree behind me." The mind must be made blank, so that an objective appraisal can be undertaken. What the reflections represent is not important. What is important is the pattern of light and dark, and the relationship of degrees of gray to absolute white or absolute black.

For simplicity's sake, the beginner makes these assumptions: there is a strip of dark across the top and down one side of the glass, which is the shadow from the frame. Second, if there is a curtain or a venetian blind behind the glass, a shadow line from the window mullions will fall on it. A tree should not be drawn in the window because a tree is being reflected there. Instead, the reflection of the tree must be reduced to abstract shapes of light and dark. Beyond that, careful observation of the light and dark values is in order.

It is wise to practice drawing reflections in both pencil and pen. Pen, as usual, forces simplicity.

Problem 88:
Reflections in windows

Use a pen and grid paper. Lay out the overall shape of the window carefully, because as it is subdivided for the panes, inaccuracies will appear magnified. Squint in order to cut down on details and to see the relative values better.

Relative values are what you will draw—what is darkest, what is lightest, without regard to what the values stand for in terms of reflection. In the end, check to make sure that you have a shadow across the top and down one side. Repeat this exercise using pencil and grid paper. (See figs. 6-50, 6-51, 6-52, 6-53, and 6-54.)

Reflections crop up on all kinds of entourage important to architects, landscape architects, and interior designers—outdoor lighting fixtures, for example, or objects in stainless steel, or metal trash containers. They can all be handled the same way: by seeing only a pattern of light and shade instead of trying to create an inside, an outside, and a surface (fig. 6-55).

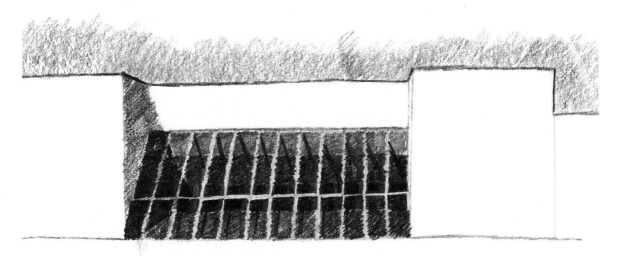

Figure 6-50

Figures 6-51, 6-52

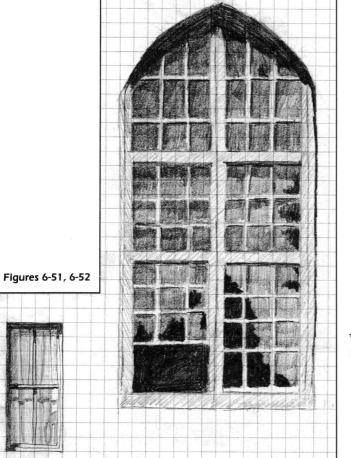

Figure 6-53

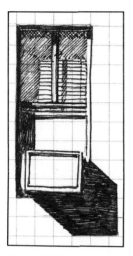

Figure 6-54

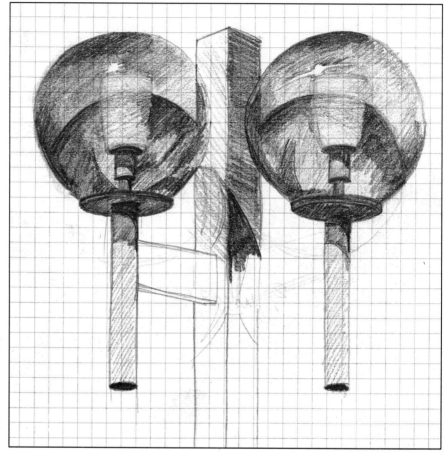

Figure 6-55

SCALE FIGURES

The subject of figure drawing is usually anathema to students, and their drawings show it. Certainly, students in the spatial professions do not have the several years of study needed to become proficient in life drawing. By the same token, it is imperative that a degree of skill be attained so that the results are not grotesque or laughable.

Again, gridded sketch paper helps immediately because it provides a scale for the size of a figure. Every tree, car, and building has a measurable size against which a person can be judged.

What kind of a person is to be drawn? It needs to be diagrammatic to a degree, because a realistic figure is beyond the capabilities of most students. The more detail that is applied to the figure to make it look real—buttons, belts, backpacks, glasses—the more trouble the student will have.

A symbolic figure is probably too simplistic for most presentation sheets, although if trees and other entourage are depicted symbolically, perhaps the people could follow suit. But the clichéd graphic symbols that are common on rest-room doors should be avoided.

One good solution is the use of outline figures (fig. 6-56). The outline should be based on real life—in other words, an outline traced from a photograph. It can be enlarged or reduced on a photocopier to achieve the desired size. This approach has several advantages. One is that the figure looks real. Moreover, it serves the purpose for which it has been created, namely to show scale and/or to imply the presence of people in architectural space. Finally, because it is only an outline, it does not draw undue attention to itself. After all, an architectural drawing is meant to illustrate a building, garden, or interior, not people.

Figure 6-56

Magazines and newspapers are full of photos suitable for tracing. A collection can be made easily and kept in a notebook.

Some professionals have devised their own trademark figures, the most famous being Le Corbusier's Modulor*. These can be interestingly misshapen, but they do not appeal to all tastes (fig. 6-57). A more conservative approach is usually a better choice.

MODULOR

Figure 6-57

*Le Corbusier created a scale based on a human figure, the proportions of which he related to the golden section.

7.

Contour

This chapter on contour, and the next chapter, on negative space, move away from formulas for drawing and methods of drawing accurately to ways of seeing that are vitally important to everyone in the spatial arts.

Architecture is a down-to-earth profession, specializing in solid material. A feel for volume is a characteristic of the architect, to whom plastic, three-dimensional forms are the essential building blocks of structure. This feeling for volume should be evident in the drawing of solids: practice in making things look solid will reinforce the subjective feeling.

We have already seen that value drawing—using light and shade—is one way of making objects look solid. *Contour drawing* is a type of line drawing that also gives objects a feeling of volume. Contour is the shape of a surface. A string laid on a plane will define its contour. Every surface has contour, no matter how flat and smooth that surface may be. It is simply a flat and smooth contour.

Drawings that emphasize contour project a sense of three-dimensional solidity. Architects and interior designers, who manipulate volumes for a living, find this kind of drawing very useful.

Contour exercises purposely direct the mind away from attention to edges, which is a flattening technique, to emphasize the modulation of surface, which makes objects look solid. Since a surface can extend in all directions, it follows that a contour also can move in any direction.

In a pure contour drawing, the final product may bear little resemblence to the object itself, since the overriding purpose of the drawing is not its looks but its feeling.

Problem 89:
Contour drawing
of a hand

Use a pencil. Grid paper is not necessary. You will use your own hand as the prop in this exercise, since it is convenient and everyone has one.

Place your hand in an interesting position beside your drawing paper. You are going to try to develop a direct connection between your eye and your drawing hand. Draw your hand, focusing your concentration on the surface that the line is imitating. Keep the pencil on the paper—do not take it off—in order to reinforce the feeling of movement in the hand that is drawing. The line may, and should, go in any direction that the contour takes it. Go *slowly*, to keep the eye and the drawing hand moving as one. As in life, it is the journey that is important, not the destination. You are journeying across your hand.

The areas of greatest activity, for example, around the knuckles, will doubtless engender the most lines. While it is true that wrinkles and folds in the skin are powerful indications of contours, do not forget that there are contours across the smooth sections as well.

The question always arises, "If I can't lift my pencil off the paper, how do I get over there?" The answer is that you move your drawing hand there in the same way that you move your eye there—by traveling across the field to get to the other side. (See fig. 7-1.)

Cautionary note: an outline of the hand is the least exciting of all possible contours. It shows minimal surface and absolutely no volume.

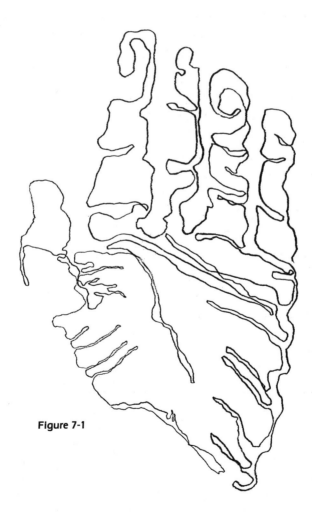

Figure 7-1

Problem 90: Contour drawing of a hand

Use a pencil. Grid paper is not necessary. Draw your right hand with your left hand. (If you are left-handed, draw your left hand with your right.) Again, keep the pencil on the paper—do not lift it. Your line should follow the progress of your eye as it explores the surface of your hand. Take all the time you need. (See fig. 7-2.)

The exercise in problem 90 will come as an eye opener to students who discover that the drawing produced by the "wrong" hand is more sensitive than that produced by their "right" hand. The brain must force the hand to do something it is not used to doing. It is bypassing the programming that has been developed through decades of habit. As with any motion that is deliberate, the result is more perceptive than that for the same motion accomplished by rote. Although the drawings are certainly distorted from a realistic point of view, they unquestionably project a response to the form that shapes the hand from the inside, as well as the wonderfully varied terrain of the surface.

Problem 91: Blind drawing of a hand

Use a pencil. Grid paper is not necessary. Lay a piece of paper over your drawing hand, anchoring it by poking the pencil end through the page (fig. 7-3). This will ensure that you cannot see what you are drawing. All your attention can be riveted on the exploration of contour by means of a line. As you draw your hand do not raise the pencil off the paper. You will probably lose your way in any event. Do not worry; continue drawing from wherever you think you are.

Problem 91 is always good for lots of laughs, both in execution and in the critiques that follow. Although the results are not as good as when drawing with the left hand, the experience of having no frame of reference is still a salutary one.

Figures 7-4 and 7-5 show pages of hands drawn by beginning students. Each page has a hand drawn by the right hand, a hand drawn by the left hand, and one drawn blind.

Figure 7-2

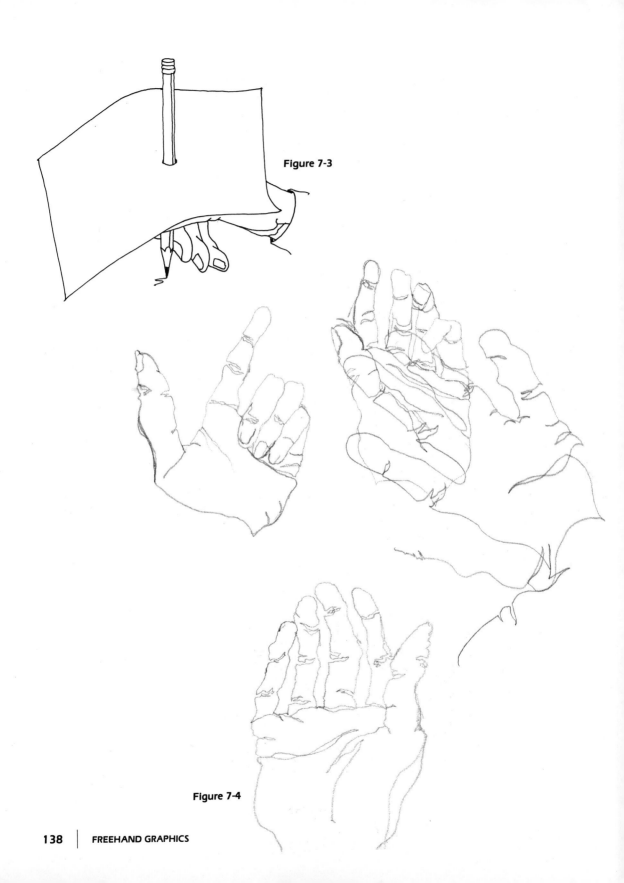

Figure 7-3

Figure 7-4

Figure 7-5

Problem 92:
Contour drawing
with no outline

Use a pencil. Grid paper is not necessary. This time you are to draw your hand without allowing your line to follow the outline of the hand at all. No line can do more than touch its outside edge. Do not simply make back-and-forth strokes across the hand—such drawing is mindless and boring.

Ideally most drawing should include contour; the concept of volume should inform all nonorthographic images. Lots of practice is needed to break the habit of outlining. In this pursuit all sorts of props can be used. Figure 7-6, for example, is a drawing of a cow skull by a beginning student. Driftwood has a rich, weblike sur-

Figure 7-6

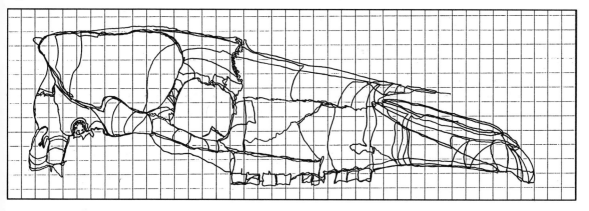

face laid over its form. And its form is like turbulent water petrified (fig. 7-7). Cars and toothpaste tubes have just as much contour as any other object (figs. 7-8 and 7-9). And faces have unlimited potential (fig. 7-10).

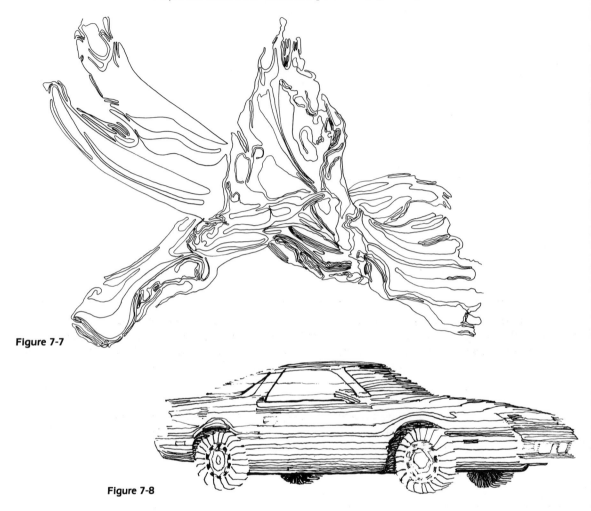

Figure 7-7

Figure 7-8

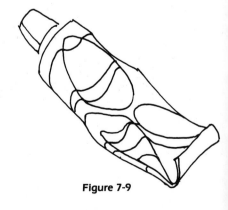

Figure 7-9

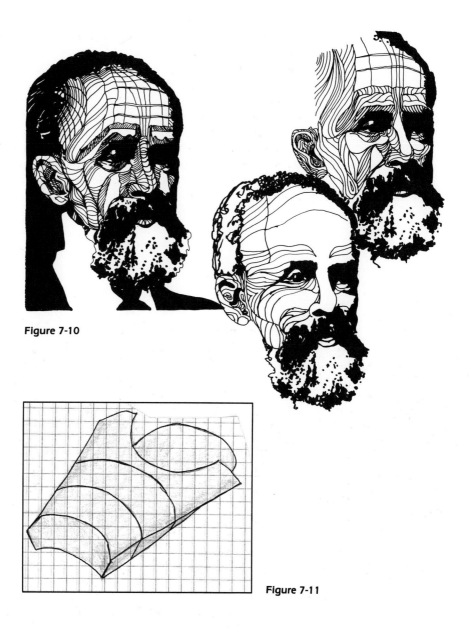

Figure 7-10

Figure 7-11

**Problem 93:
Contour in a
limited number
of lines**

Use a pencil. Grid paper is not necessary. Draw a fast-food french fry container using only five or six lines. It must show the concave bottom and the convex front and back as well as the shapely outline. (See fig. 7-11.)

Cautionary note: contour lines start at an edge and continue until reaching another edge. Little isolated lines that look like pieces of spaghetti provide no hint of contour.

Using contour in drawing outdoors can help in the analysis of a site, by isolating individual units. Producing vertical contours, as in a loaf of sliced bread, is one technique. A slice is taken every few feet along the scene, going through the most important elements (fig. 7-12). More interesting is a staggered and selective slicing (fig. 7-13).

"Bread-slice" contours are useful for practice; but a flexible line contour should become part and parcel of all sketching. There should be contour lines under all trees, firmly rooting them to the ground (fig. 7-14). Contour lines should be used in any large open space, such as parking lots, mowed lawns, and expanses of tarmac. Why? To break up the space, so that it is not monotonous, allowing the mind's eye to have something to follow.

Figure 7-12

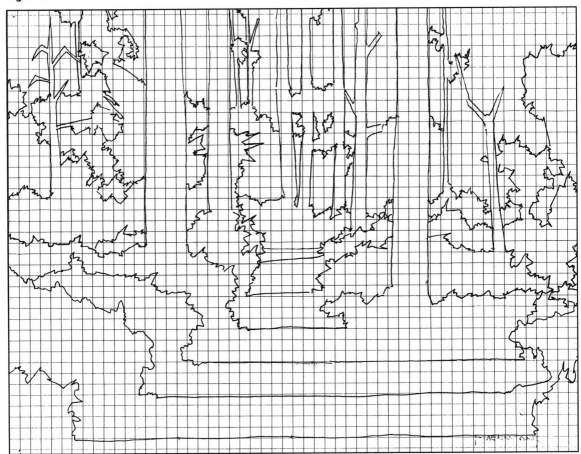

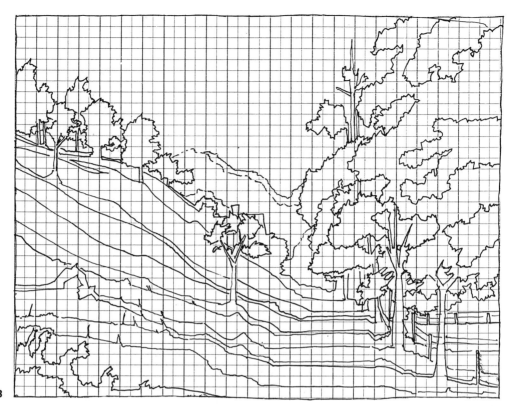

Figure 7-13

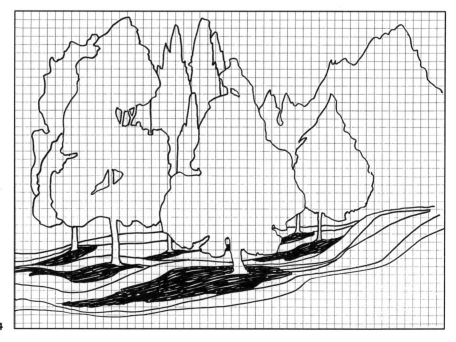

Figure 7-14

8.

Negative Space

Whereas contour drawing is a means of showing volume as an enclosure, drawing negative space is a way of considering space as a volume. Because architects and interior designers use space as their artistic medium, shaping it and molding it to match their unique vision, students should cultivate the habit of experiencing the space surrounding them and actively responding to its presence.

To draw negative space is first to see, in an almost physical sense, the space within, the space without, or the space surrounding a solid.

Problem 94: Negative-space drawing of stripes

Use a pen on tracing paper. A striped fabric (a flag works well) will be draped over an inverted stool or chair.

On your tracing paper, draw only the white stripes, isolating them from their surroundings. Follow the outside edges of the stripe.

Squinting a lot is a splendid way of eliminating the less important wrinkles and shadows and allowing the shape of the stripes to show. Do not draw lines where white stripes cross each other. Each stripe or combination of stripes will be a single unit when completed. (See fig. 8-1.)

On another piece of tracing paper, the same size as the first, draw only the colored stripes. Do not try to match the two sheets. If the first drawing was too small on the page, or in other respects was not pleasing, do better on the second one. (See fig. 8-2.)

Now superimpose the two drawings. Any mismatching of the two will make an interesting new drawing. Move the two drawings in all directions. Turn one over, and move them around again. Are the parts functioning together in some interesting way?

Something about the combination of these shapes contains an explosive quality. Exploit the nature of the design by assigning it a title, such as "The Destruction of the Natural Order" or "Disintegration of Contemporary Society." When your solution pleases you and suggests your title, trace the combined drawings onto another piece of tracing paper.

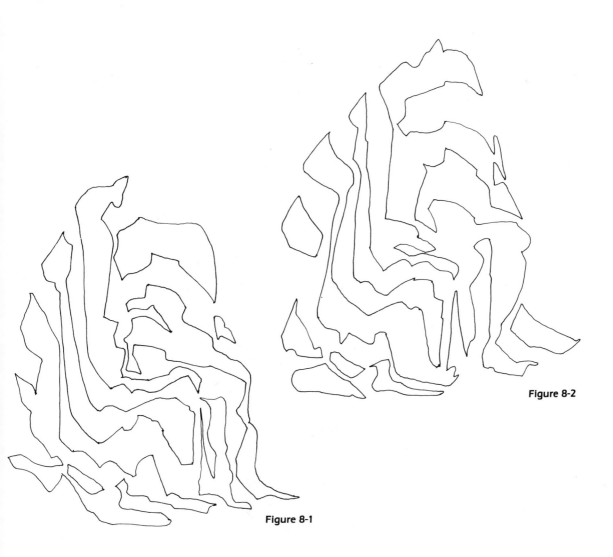

Figure 8-2

Figure 8-1

Problem 95:
Rendering of
negative space

Use a pen. Render the finally traced drawing from problem 94 by filling in some or all of the spaces that have been created with parallel lines, with light and shade, with color. All choices should be made to support the theme of disintegration. (See fig. 8-3.)

A full-fledged negative-space problem requires a more complex setup. I frequently use a collection of easels, propped up on a table. The rule is to draw *only* the space around them. Any reference to the wood of the easels will spoil concentration on the space.

Each negative space must be seen as a polygon of a certain size and shape and drawn accurately before moving to the next shape. Each shape must be seen individually, not as part of a greater whole. Properly drawn, no shape will touch any other.

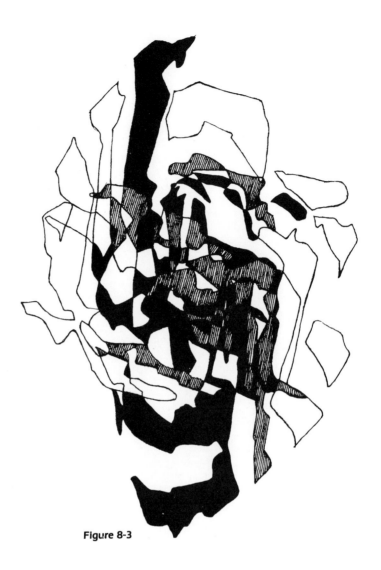

Figure 8-3

**Problem 96:
Negative-space
drawing of
easels**

Use a pen. Grid paper is not necessary. Start with a clearly defined area of space somewhere in the middle of the composition. The drawing will become increasingly less accurate as you work outward, and starting in the middle means you have less distance to any given side. If you begin to get out of sync, it does not matter; just move to the next shape.

One problem that will arise is what to do at the outside edges—it is all too easy to find yourself just drawing a line around the profile of the easels. One solution is to bring a line in arbitrarily from the edge of the paper, creating the feeling that you are bringing space with it. (See fig. 8-4.)

When a negative-space drawing is finished, it is truly finished—rarely is it improved with tinkering. Instead, it can be turned into a new challenge, seen with

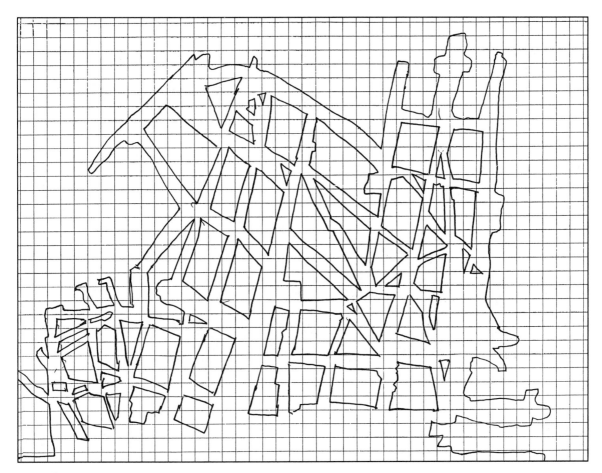

Figure 8-4

new eyes. Negative spaces that have become positive spaces can be shaded, or they can be filled in with texture. A totally new graphic can be created—it is a problem in two-dimensional design that demands a consideration of the whole page as well as the design. The page should always be part of the grand plan.

Figures 8-5, 8-6, 8-7, and 8-8 are four superior student solutions to the problem. Each conveys a very different feeling.

A negative-space drawing will result in a graphic that has an unusual and appealing sense of the surreal. When using props that have all straight lines, the resulting drawing will remind one of the plan of a medieval city (fig. 8-9).

Figure 8-10 is a plan of the medieval city of Martina Franca, in Italy. The resemblance to the negative-space drawing is too close to neglect. Studying the negative-space drawing, let us imagine descending into a medieval city and looking around.

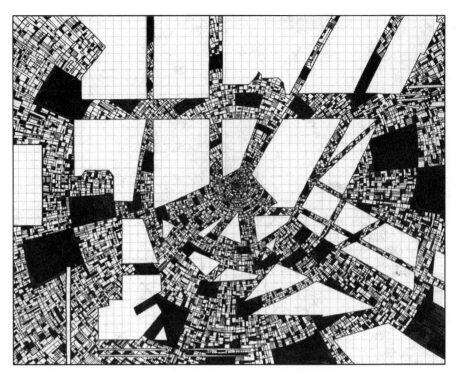

Figure 8-5

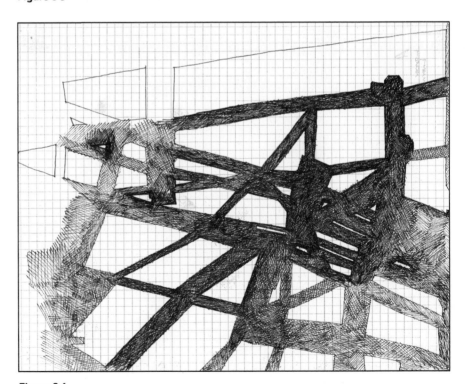

Figure 8-6

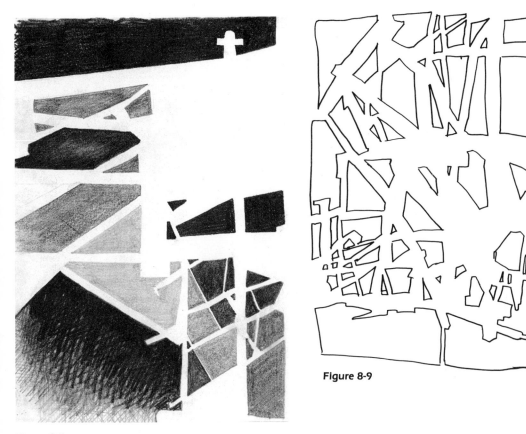

Figure 8-7

Figure 8-8

Figure 8-9

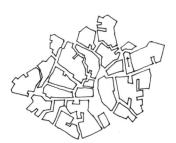

Figure 8-10

**Problem 97:
Plan oblique on
a negative-space
drawing**

Use a pencil and grid paper. Using the negative-space drawing from problem 95, imagine it as the plan of a medieval city. Imagine a building on each of the polygons. Look up and down the narrow streets and into the piazzas. Be a city planner. Think big. Pick an interesting view, and draw a cityscape.

Draw your buildings as plan obliques; in other words, turn the corner of one of the polygons toward you before raising the verticals.

Keep all shapes geometric in form. Include no windows with curtains or other details that would indicate human use. Some of the polygons can be left in outline—they will look like planting beds. Vary the heights of the geometric solids to lend excitement to the composition.

Work out the entire composition with pencil on scratch paper before beginning the final drawing, which should be done in ink. (See figs. 8-11 and 8-12.)

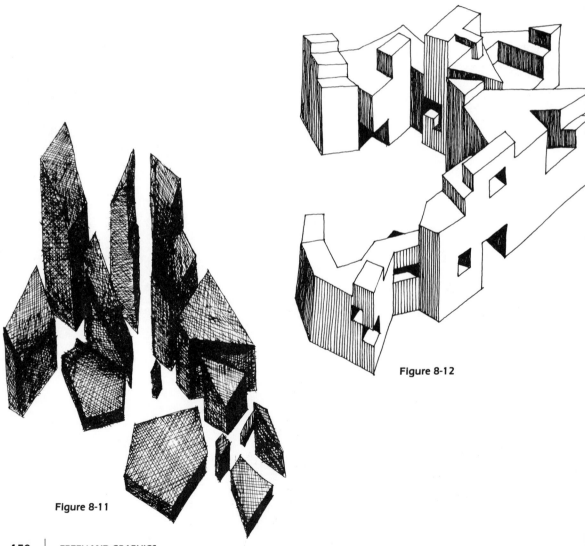

Figure 8-12

Figure 8-11

**Problem 98:
Change of scale
in a city drawing**

Use a pen and grid paper. Trace problem 97 (the medieval city) onto a new sheet of paper. Change the scale drastically by adding something to the composition: a hand, for example, to shrink the apparent size of the city. Whatever you choose to add, draw it in contour so that a nice variety in styles results. Work out the new composition in pencil before rendering it in ink. (See figs. 8-13 and 8-14.)

Many objects make beguiling negative-space compositions for practice purposes—spiky bushes, old umbrellas, piles of chairs (figs. 8-15 and 8-16). Practice in seeing space will be richly rewarding, both for drawing ability and for a long-range response to space as a volume.

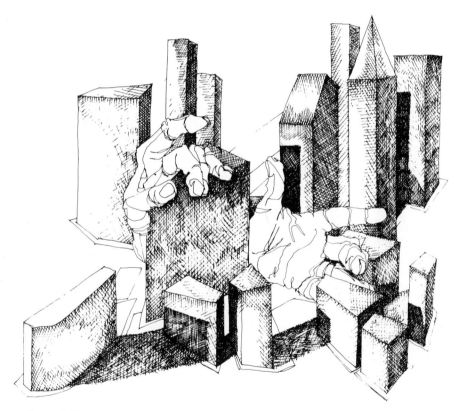

Figure 8-13

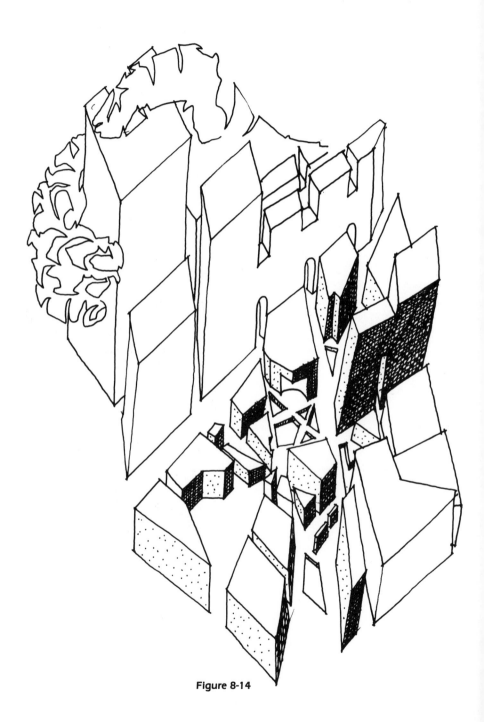

Figure 8-14

Figure 8-15

Figure 8-16

Conclusion

Drawing, as described in this book, is a means to an end more than it is an end in itself. It is the successful transfer of thought from mind to paper in a pleasing and accurate manner.

Confidence and competence in drawing are not only essential for presentation sheets but will go a long way toward improving the quality of an individual's design capabilities, if for no other reason than that all effort can be funneled into the creative endeavor.

More than that, chances are good that in becoming skillful, you will also discover another delightful means of communication, a way of expressing the world around you in a uniquely personal manner. Drawing is a stamp as individual as a fingerprint. Master it not just for its usefulness but for its pleasure.

Illustration Credits

Grateful acknowledgment is made to the University of Arkansas Department of Architecture for permission to use the classroom work shown in this book. All of the following drawings were done by students. (Figures in parenthesis indicate the size in inches of the sheet used if larger than $8^1/2$ by 11.)

1-2. Jason Jones ($17^1/2$ by $22^1/2$)	5-12. Lee Teague
1-3. Greg Goggans ($17^1/2$ by $22^1/2$)	5-23. Shannon Perry
1-4. David Waldron ($17^1/2$ by $22^1/2$)	5-24. Jason Jones
1-5. Unidentified	5-25. Roger Schrader
1-6. Lancer Livermont	5-27. Jason Hayes
2-2. JoAnn Teas (18 by 93)	5-28. Jason Hayes
2-6. Lee Teague	5-29. Lee Teague
2-7. Paul Carter	5-30. Joel Dodson ($13^3/4$ by 17)
2-8. Unidentified	5-31. Lee Teague
2-14. Chad Eby	5-32. Unidentified
2-15. Chad Eby	6-6. Joel Dodson
2-18. Tracy Spillman	6-7. Wesley Garrett
2-42. Rick Rogers ($13^3/4$ by 17)	6-8. Unidentified
2-49. David Lewis ($9^1/2$ by 13)	6-9. Unidentified
2-50. JoAnn Teas	6-10. Unidentified
2-51. Mary Sanders ($9^3/4$ by $13^1/2$)	6-11. Unidentified
2-55. Unidentified	6-12. Brian Wray
2-56. Lee Teague	6-13. Lee Teague
2-57. Lee Teague	6-14. Lee Teague
2-58. Lee Teague	6-15. Ed Fusco
2-59. JoAnn Teas	6-16. Lee Teague
2-60. JoAnn Teas	6-17. Eric Johnson
2-61. JoAnn Teas	6-18. Brian Wray
3-8. David Olsen	6-19. Brian Wethington
3-9. Lancer Livermont	6-20. Jason Hayes
3-10. Dale Walden	6-27. Allen Arnn
3-12. Dale Walden (11 by 14)	6-28. Greg Goggans
3-13. Lancer Livermont (10 by 14)	6-29. Lancer Livermont
3-16. Dale Walden	6-32. Greg Goggans
3-17. Dale Walden	6-35. Patty Fairman (14 by 17)
4-22. Joe Rose	6-36. Betty Loewer (12 by $13^1/4$)

Index